THE
COACHING
BIBLE

Other books by Ian McDermott

The NLP Coach (with Wendy Jago)
Your Inner Coach (with Wendy Jago)
Way of NLP (with Joseph O'Connor)
First Directions NLP (with Joseph O'Connor)
Manage Yourself, Manage Your Life (with Ian Shircore)
Practical NLP for Managers (with Joseph O'Connor)
NLP and the New Manager (with Ian Shircore)
NLP and Health (with Joseph O'Connor)
Brief NLP Therapy (with Wendy Jago)
The Art of Systems Thinking (with Joseph O'Connor)
Develop Your Leadership Qualities (with Joseph O'Connor et al)
Take Control of Your Life (with Joseph O'Connor et al)

Coaching CDs by Ian McDermott

Essential Coaching Skills
How to Coach Yourself
Spiritual Dimension of Coaching
The Power to Change
Professional Development Programme
Your Best Year Yet!

Other books by Wendy Jago

Brief NLP Therapy (with Ian McDermott)
The NLP Coach (with Ian McDermott)
Your Inner Coach (with Ian McDermott)
Effective Communication in Practice (with Jan Pye)

Equestrian titles by Wendy Jago
Schooling Problems Solved with NLP
Solo Schooling: Learn to Coach Yourself when You're Riding Alone

THE
COACHING
BIBLE

THE ESSENTIAL HANDBOOK

IAN MCDERMOTT & WENDY JAGO

PIATKUS

Copyright © 2005 by Ian McDermott and Wendy Jago

First published in Great Britain in 2005 by
Piatkus Books Ltd
5 Windmill Street
London W1T 2JA
e-mail: info@piatkus.co.uk

This edition published in 2006

The quote by Peter Senge on p. 27 is reprinted by permission of the Random House Group.

The quote on p. 114 is reprinted by permission of HarperCollins Publishers Ltd © Guy Claxton, 1998.

Every effort has been made to seek permission for the use of all quotations used throughout this book.

The moral right of the authors has been asserted

A catalogue record for this book is available from the British Library

ISBN 0 7499 2704 6

Text design by Paul Saunders

This book has been printed on paper manufactured with respect for the environment using wood from managed sustainable resources

Typeset by Action Publishing Technology Ltd, Gloucester
Printed and bound in Great Britain by
William Clowes Ltd, Beccles, Suffolk

About the Authors

Ian McDermott and Wendy Jago are the authors of the definitive books *The NLP Coach* and *Your Inner Coach*.

Ian McDermott was recently named one of Britain's Top 10 Coaches and described as 'the coaches' coach' (*Independent on Sunday*). Coach, consultant and international trainer, he is one of the world's foremost exponents of NLP Coaching. Ian coaches many FTSE and Fortune 500 clients around the world and works personally with key senior players focusing on strategic issues, creativity and innovation. His work is also featured in the Open University MBA programme 'Creativity, Innovation and Change'. He is the founder of International Teaching Seminars (ITS) which is the world's premier NLP Coaching organisation. Co-author of 12 best-selling books which have been translated into 15 languages, Ian spends much of his time training the next generation of coaches.

Wendy Jago is a coach, consultant and author. She has a diploma in hypnosis and psychotherapy and is an NLP Master Practitioner and certified coach. She has pioneered the application of NLP and coaching to equestrian training through her books *Schooling Problems Solved with NLP* and *Solo Schooling*, and enjoys working with both riders and international executives. She also co-authored *Brief NLP Therapy* with Ian McDermott.

Dedication

For Jan Elfline

Contents

Acknowledgements

We would like to salute all those who have contributed to the evolution of what today is commonly called coaching. Our special thanks to Jan Elfline, Pam Richarde, Jeff Staggs and Laura Whitworth.

Thanks too to the Piatkus team of Gill Bailey for her wise editorial input and Helen Stanton for helping us make this happen.

SECTION 1: The Heart and Soul of Coaching

Introduction

> *Coaching is unlocking a person's potential to maximise their own performance. It is helping them to learn rather than teaching them. We are more like an acorn, which contains within it all the potential to be a magnificent oak tree. We need nourishment, encouragement and the light to reach towards, but the oaktreeness is already within.*

John Whitmore, *Coaching for Performance*, Nicholas Brealey, 1996, pages 8–9

Suppose you were offered a way to recognise and realise your goals, to find and utilise your unique strengths, to manage yourself more effectively, to identify and work around your limitations, to focus your intention and your resources and, above all, to make changes in your life for the better. Would you be interested? This is what coaching has to offer.

Nowadays there is a substantial literature on coaching. However, we believe we have something both unique and valuable to offer you if:

- You are thinking about getting a coach.
- You commission coaching for others.
- You're thinking of becoming a coach.
- You're already a coach and looking to extend your skills.

- You're not interested in actually becoming a coach, but want to learn how to adopt a coaching approach in everyday life.

Though these are clearly different orientations and roles there is an extraordinary amount of overlap in what matters for people in any of them. A good coaching approach offers the same benefits even when starting points and perspectives differ. This is why we will use the word 'you' so often in this book without specifying, 'you the client', 'you the coach' or 'you the commissioner'. When what we're saying applies to one role in particular we will of course make clear which role.

The Coaching Bible is a comprehensive guide to the key issues and processes that make coaching one of the most powerful and exciting tools for furthering personal and professional effectiveness. This is not a book that is just for coaches, or potential clients, or commissioners of coaching for others. Because we look at coaching as an approach, it is for anyone who seeks to gain, or help develop, greater personal mastery.

We want you to have access to the best there is available. To that end, we intend to equip you with the right tools to enable you to ask the right questions, make informed judgements and find a path through the plethora of competing models and 'latest approaches'. We will give you a map that is both authoritative and inclusive because it rests on best practice, tried and tested by many coaches with different backgrounds in different contexts. We tell you what works, how it works and why it works.

In our view coaching is more than a set of skills: it is a different way of being, one that characterises excellent coaches whatever their particular training or style. It comes from a profound coherence between what the coach does, what they believe and who they are. This is what makes good coaching seamless in practice. It's what lies behind its power to help people make changes and in the process discover more of what they have it in them to become.

The internal consistency of the coach and the way they exercise their skills is what distinguishes good coaching from its indifferent look-alikes. *The Coaching Bible* demonstrates this consistency by taking you through a comprehensive model that anyone can use, whether they are a coach, client or commissioner of coaching for others. This model will also be really useful if you simply want to employ a coaching *approach* in everyday life – as many managers are now being called upon to do. The core of this book, and of our approach to coaching, is not a model that attempts to be different from others that you may encounter, but one that underpins and explains the effectiveness of all the rest.

In offering you this way of understanding we are not claiming to have invented something new: rather, we are seeking to reveal a structure that underlies *all* good coaching. Michelangelo once said that the task of the sculptor is to reveal the statue hidden within the stone. To do so he must remove the fragments of stone concealing what is within and so reveal its true essence. That's what *The Coaching Bible* seeks to do for coaching.

We offer you many how-tos, but they are put forward within this guiding template of coaching's essential core. We are not promoting a formula that has to be followed slavishly. People seeking to use a formula often find that they are trying to make themselves and others fit the formula – as an experienced colleague of ours once said, 'The client is so often the victim of the last training you took.' What we are doing is inviting you to develop your own style and your own way of participating in coaching, whether it's as a coach, client or commissioner, or just if you want to employ a coaching approach in your everyday life.

The Coaching Bible models our own belief: that it is as essential to be human in coaching as it is to be professional, and that the way to do this is to accept and learn to work with what actually happens rather than what 'should happen'. The essential ingredient that translates this into professionalism rather than mere pragmatism is our MultiModal Coaching template, which we explore in depth in Chapter 2.

Using an underlying and inclusive template has another advantage, too. You don't have to struggle to 'get it right'. Learning to coach is like learning to manage your life: you don't have to be perfect, only to manage as best you can, with commitment, integrity, humility – and often humour. We've found that the MultiModal template seems to give people a clear understanding of their role in the coaching partnership. Our aim, therefore, is for you to have a clearer understanding of just what is involved, so that your choices will be better informed and the actions you take will be most appropriately and effectively targeted.

Effectiveness comes in many forms and involves the use of many tools. We look for the elements that are often or always present and for the tools that invariably work. This inclusiveness means that we can distil the essence of coaching and present its primary tools so they are accessible not just for coaches and those who wish to have coaching skills, but also for anyone who wants to benefit from good coaching.

Coaching and ourselves

Naturally, as a reader you will want to know something about us – not just about our experience, but also what kind of people we are. Will you get along with us? Will we be the right people to help you, here and now, get the most from working together?

We are both professional coaches with a lot of experience in coaching itself, as well as in other helping roles. We have both worked as therapists and trainers, sharing a belief in the ability of every individual we work with to know what they want, and in their potential resourcefulness to work towards achieving it.

Ian is one of the world's leading trainers of coaches and a coach himself. He is the founder and Director of Training of International Teaching Seminars. He has trained many thousands of people to practitioner and master practitioner level in NLP and is co-developer of the first NLP Coaching certification programme officially accredited by coaching's international body, the International Coach Federation. As one of the first cohort of students to take that programme, Wendy thinks she probably received the best coaching training in the world, one that added a new dimension to her existing skills. Together, we have written several highly successful books on coaching. We love what we do and from our experience of its effects we believe wholeheartedly in its worth.

Because we have been involved in both teaching and therapy, and between us have a range of training and experience to draw upon, we've done enough to know the difference between coaching and other forms of helping, and this forms an important strand of this book. Although widely used, the term 'coaching' doesn't yet carry a consistency of meaning, and this leads to confusion and sometimes misunderstandings among professionals as well as among potential clients. We aim to clarify just what coaching really consists of.

As experienced coaches, we recognise the value not just of coaching itself, but also of a coaching approach. This can be employed by just about anyone – not just coaches. It is a way of building greater effectiveness and quality control into all relationships that involve support, control and influence. In fact, we believe that most relationships can benefit from such a coaching approach – whether you are a friend, a parent, a child, a teacher, a pupil, a professional, a colleague or a client. As we've discovered in our own lives, all the skills this book explores, all the values upon which it rests – and the way of being that underpins them – can apply in every sphere of life.

One final point while we are talking about us: a good question to ask anyone who claims to be a coach is, 'Do you have a coach?' Do we, in fact, ourselves have coaching? Of course we do. If it's so good why wouldn't we want some too? How much would you trust the purveyor of any product or service if they didn't value it enough to use it themselves? So beware those who think coaching is only for others. Conversely, how much more would you trust them if they could demonstrate how it enriched their lives, not just once, not just in the past, not just in specific moments of crisis, but every day, in good times as well as hard times? We each have a coach and receive regular coaching. We choose to pay for this service because we benefit hugely from it.

Why 'The Coaching *Bible*'?

This book is called *The Coaching Bible*. It is not called *The Coaching Encyclopedia*. For us a bible is something of a handbook and has a practical dimension. An encyclopedia on the other hand attempts to offer an all-encompassing, even definitive, account of its field. We would not presume to do this, not least because the field is too young. A bible though is possible.

The word bible is an interesting one. It comes from the Greek and means 'a collection of writings'. In the case of the Bible these writings are the fruits of many people and multiple perspectives accreted over time. In everyday parlance the word has certain connotations. A book referred to as the bible in its field is authoritative, a source of reference and, potentially, guidance. Too often, though, people want to use such texts to legitimate a particular doctrinal view. When this happens, whether it's in the field of religion, psychotherapy, organisational theory or whatever, these documents become hostage to 'the only way folk', those who want to render the world simple by asserting that there is only one truth and that – surprise, surprise – they just happen to be in sole possession of it.

Such fearful fundamentalism is diametrically opposed to coaching. There are many ways of doing outstanding coaching. Equally there are many different – and valid – perspectives on it. However, this does not mean that there are no core elements uniting apparently different approaches and practitioners. In the same vein, there *are* standards of excellence and best practice that we shall be going into in depth.

The inclusiveness of coaching doesn't imply a woolly 'anything goes' approach. That's the very opposite of the rigour that goes with the coaching process. It would also be quite at odds with the demands of what in coaching is known as accountability (see page 102). Authoritativeness also has its place in coaching. However, it has to be earned. In our experience, the authority of the coach rests as much on their humanity as upon their skills. Coaching is, above all, an ongoing process of management and leadership: of self just as much as of the external world, and of the coach by the coach just as much as of the client by the client.

We seek to offer you an account of coaching that is authoritative and comprehensive while rejecting the claim that ours is the 'only' or 'best' way. Very often people assume that when something is authoritative it's the last word on the subject. We confidently predict the opposite. *The Coaching Bible* is not the last word on coaching. Nonetheless, we do believe that we offer a way of understanding the processes and values involved in coaching that will continue to be of value because it gladly embraces both new tools and new thinking. This is because we address the essentials that do not change.

Because best practice continues to develop in coaching, as in any profession, we fully expect that other skilled professionals will have different views, many of which will enhance or complement what we have to say – and we expect to continue developing our own thinking. This happens in coaching itself. A coach can have a view and be authoritative, without necessarily being either exclusive or excluding. So this bible has space in it for more that has yet to be discovered.

What does this book offer you?

- It shows you how to find your own way in a complex field. It clarifies what coaching is and what it's not.

- It teaches you about coaching and its relevance for you in ways that are akin to coaching itself.

- It is inclusive – it doesn't rule out things by saying they are 'not relevant' but rather asks '*how* is this relevant?' You will therefore find yourself becoming a better questioner and a deeper enquirer as you read.

- It tolerates and can handle paradoxes and even contradiction. Life is a lot easier to manage when we don't try to make it too simple.

- It will help you make new connections. It respects and includes body language and tone as much as verbal content, beliefs as much as actions, confidence and confidences as much as fears and secrets.

- Through our comprehensive MultiModal template it offers you a way of understanding just what it is you are dealing with and how it connects with the rest of your life.

- It gives you the benefits of a *systemic* understanding of actions and reactions, meanings and strategies, enabling you to act more effectively with those around you – and with yourself.

- Through examples drawn from many different kinds of coaching situations, and from the perspective of coach, client and commissioner, it ensures that you will find plenty that is relevant to your situation and your needs.

- It takes into account different ways of thinking and different points of view, helping you relate detail and the bigger picture more effectively, regardless of which perspective you naturally take.

- It gives you tools you can use in both formal and informal situations.

- It models the beliefs, values and processes that it's talking about, so that you get a sense of what it's like to be involved in a coaching partnership for real.

Introducing Coaching

'Coaching is the facilitation of learning and development with the purpose of improving performance and enhancing effective action, goal achievement and personal satisfaction. It invariably involves growth and change, whether that is in perspective, attitude or behaviour.'

Peter Bluckert, *The Foundations of a Psychological Approach to Executive Coaching*, (www.pbcoaching.com)

We came across this definition on a coach's website. And, as definitions go, we think it's rather good. Given the kind of work we do, our own definition would be, 'Coaching is a conversational yet focused discipline that supports people in learning how to lead and manage themselves more effectively in relation to their issues, their resources, their contexts and their potential.' But if you want to understand coaching, how it works and what it offers, definitions won't get you very far. Like so many human experiences, defining coaching is a poor substitute for experiencing it. Here therefore in introducing coaching we want to go beyond definition and give you a flavour of the activity itself. If at any time you want to review what are generally thought of as the key coaching competencies you will find these summarised in the Appendix (see page 177).

Throughout this book we have given specific examples drawn from our clients' experiences. We have chosen those which are most representative of so many people's experience – so issues like weight loss will certainly figure more than once. Identities and personal details have been changed to preserve people's confidentiality.

At its heart, coaching is about partnership – not just the obvious one between client and coach, but also partnerships between reason and emotion, reflection and action. Coaching is interactive: it is a dialogue between equals. It involves a pooling of expertise. The client is the expert on herself and her situation and the coach is the expert on helping her discover how to make the changes she wants to make in her work and other parts of her life.

Coaching recognises that small changes, if properly targeted, can have far-reaching results. That's why the best coaches are experts on leverage. It is, however, concerned primarily with process rather than actual content. It is marked by clarity in some areas: clarity of purpose, role, boundaries and ways and means. It's also characterised by open-endedness in other areas because of the need for inquiry, exploration, reflection and experimentation. It is a process that is highly tolerant of doubt and ambiguity, and yet at the same time sharply focused.

If we were to characterise the flavour of coaching we'd say it is generous without being indulgent, focused without excluding, exploratory without becoming discursive. It is rigorous, systematic, enquiring, task related, profound yet humorous. It can be exciting, touching, strenuous and exhilarating – and all this sometimes in a single session.

Coaching is all about learning – for the coach as well as for the client. Each coaching partnership is unique, making its own operating rules, its own discoveries and its own journey of progress. The best coaching takes no prisoners and pulls no punches, yet it develops the clients' acceptance of themselves and others.

Over time we've noticed that coaching becomes habitual – not because its conversations continue indefinitely, but because its patterns of reflection, enquiry, experiment and evaluation transfer from the coach to the client. It becomes part of the client's own way of dealing with their experience. It also becomes a way of thinking that can cascade through organisations and families.

In the past the key attributes of coaching have characterised many different kinds of successful relationships. Over the last 20 years or so these attributes have been distilled into a body of knowledge and a set of tools that can be systematically learnt. Now they can be used by anyone in a wide variety of personal and organisational settings. We want to show you how.

Before we go much further it's probably going to be useful to make some distinctions; in particular to distinguish between formal and informal coaching and between executive and life coaching.

Formal and Informal Coaching

Formal coaching often begins with an initial intake or foundation appointment. The coach and client set up a regular meeting or call schedule. They agree the length of each session, say thirty minutes. The client commits to some minimum period of time during which they will work with their coach. This becomes part of the coaching contract between the two parties.

With informal coaching coaching *skills* are used without the process taking place necessarily being labelled as coaching. These skills may have developed quite naturally. Some people have learnt the power of silence. Some have learnt not to proffer advice or rush to a 'solution'. Others have learned to listen, elicit and then focus attention on what seems most important to the speaker. All of these are coaching skills. These can also be quite deliberately learnt and improved. Such coaching skills have wide application. They can be just as effectively applied in a 10-minute chat with a colleague as they can in a pre-arranged formally labelled coaching session. Equally they are invaluable if you want to be the best parent you can be.

Executive Coaching

Often those who seek Executive Coaching are outstanding in one or more areas of life, but they want more, including some support. Sometimes they can't go any further unless they expand their skills. Perhaps they are highly successful at work but they feel they need to 'get a life' once they leave the office. Or they may be performing well at work, but recent promotion has meant there is one area – such as people skills – where they need to improve their performance. What makes Executive Coaching so attractive is that it can offer tailor-made interventions for that particular individual.

Executive Coaching is able to help executives and managers:

- gain clarity in their thinking

- change limiting beliefs

- become a support rather than a threat

- become more productive, effective and creative

- bring out the talent and potential of their teams

- improve results for clients and their own team.

A distinction is sometimes made between executive and life coaching, but in truth there is a lot of overlap between the two. After all what executive doesn't also want to have a life?

Life Coaching

Life Coaching is concerned with living your life in keeping with what's important to you. It enables you to first take stock and get clear, second regain control and third achieve balance in your life. It addresses all manner of issues; Where am I now? Where am I going? What do I want? How do I resolve this particular issue? How do I sort out my confusing and stressful life? Which career path should I pursue?
Life Coaching is able to help clients:

- take stock and then stay on track

- clarify their outcomes and what they need to do to achieve them

- develop deeper rapport and trust with themselves and others

- make steady progress towards goals by providing ongoing structure and accountability.

Benefits of a Coaching Approach

The primary skill of coaching is not to think you know the solutions but to elicit them from the real expert – your client. So often people assume that if you can just get the other person to take your advice and do as you tell them problems will be resolved. But how often do people really take others' advice? And would it have been the best solution anyway?

There are many ways of coaching. You may be formally coaching one of your people during a one-hour session but you might also be using a coaching *approach* during breakfast with your children.

Whatever your role there are real benefits to a coaching approach:

- It frees you from the tyranny of thinking you need to have it all figured out and know the answer to everything.

- You increase your influence – a coaching style invariably builds more rapport which means you find out what is *really* going on and avoid triggering resistance.

- It gives you tools to find out what's really important.

- It can be a powerful tool in encouraging greater self-reliance be it in the client or in subordinates as they learn to think for themselves more.

- It can move individual and team thinking from short-term fixes to long-term generative solutions.

- It unleashes the power of incremental change – massive cumulative change can be achieved through consistent improvement over time.

- It can clarify for each member how their work relates to team objectives – if a whole team is consistently advancing in the right direction they travel a long way.

- It promotes curiosity and creates a useful questioning culture.

- It encourages more seeking out of what's important to an individual or, in business, to one's clients.

Coaching, be it formal or informal, executive or life coaching, can be of benefit to most members of the community. Good coaches have a natural ability to enable clients to take stock, clarify their purpose, become focused and achieve greater ease. These are also the foundation of coaching *skills*. Just about anybody who is working with others will be more effective if they can do this. Hence the value of a coaching approach.

Coaching has become popular because it can deliver a lot. It offers people a way of dealing with important issues in a non-threatening way. Word of mouth referral means people see and hear the results that colleagues and friends have achieved from working with a coach. Coaching works from the empowering premise that we have the resources we need within us – but that often we would benefit from some outside assistance to help us access them. Most people go through life realising only a part of their potential and sensing that there is so much more they are capable of. Coaching offers a means for unleashing this latent potential. As people become busier, prioritising their lives becomes an increasing challenge. We have so many commitments, we don't always successfully prioritise our commitments. One of the reasons coaching has become so popular is that a coach holds us to our deadlines, our commitments and our promises. By working with a coach, we make a commitment to *ourselves*.

Coaching has arrived as a profession, and like all professions, it has good, bad and indifferent practitioners. We assume that the majority of coaches want to be good coaches; that most clients are ready to commit energy to the process; and that most organisational commissioners genuinely intend the process to deliver the best to its twin beneficiaries, the employee and the employer. We believe that the growing market for coaching and for books and courses on coaching reflects these intentions.

At the same time, we are aware of so-called coaches who operate more like counsellors, therapists and mentors; commissioners who are torn between competing loyalties; organisations which view coaching as a means to 'fix' weaknesses rather than to enhance or utilise strengths; and clients who would rather be given a 'to-do' list than engage in rigorous self-reflection, or the strenuous daily commitment of time and energy needed to achieve what they really want.

Wherever you start from, we believe this book can serve you. It comes out of our personal experience of the different partnering roles and our detailed observation of excellent coaches in many walks of life. We want to share with you our excitement and our enthusiasm, and to show you what is central and what works in coaching – and why. We hope that *The Coaching Bible* will, in its own way, become your coach about coaching.

Chapter One

What's the Point of Coaching, and What Makes it Different?

> *Coaching, you see, is not telling people what to do; it's giving them a chance to examine what they are doing in the light of their intentions.*
>
> James Flaherty, *Coaching: Evoking Excellence in Others*, Butterworth Heinemann, 1999, page xii

Why would you seek coaching, for yourself or for someone else? Ultimately because you're seeking one of two benefits – you want more or different: more of what's good or different from what you've got. Frequently it'll turn out to involve both. Either way, something will need to change. And coaching is the most versatile form of helping, for coach, commissioner and client.

Why choose coaching rather than another form of help? Different kinds of help deliver different benefits. So it's useful to match what you want with the right tool for the job. If you have issues from the past, painful feelings or interpersonal conflicts to sort out, counselling or therapy may be the most effective way to go. If you need to learn or develop a particular skill, you might seek out specific training. If, on the other hand, you want ongoing guidance while on-the-job and input from someone who has specific subject expertise you'd probably really benefit from having a mentor. This subject expertise is *the* difference between a mentor and a coach. If you want to become a superb mother or managing director you'll probably want your mentor to be one already. By contrast, you could benefit from fantastic coaching from a coach who wasn't either.

Often coaching is chosen because it commits to rapid results. Sometimes coaching suggests itself because it's not entirely clear what's needed to sort things out or to help someone already doing well to really start performing. Either way coaching is a superb tool for unpacking and clarifying. It delivers by using particular tools, which are outlined in Section 2. Equally important, it is based on equality: the expertise of the coach is a skill in the process of helping, rather than an expertise in a particular body of knowledge. In contracting with a coach, you are retaining – even highlighting – your power to choose what to focus on, and to decide what course of action to take.

Coaches assist, challenge and encourage rather than direct, advise or teach. A coach will not tell you what you should do, or how you should do it. Not only will you yourself work out what you want and choose how to go about it, but also in the process you'll learn more about what motivates you and what gets in your way. You'll also begin to develop skills for self-management that go far beyond the issue that started you on your journey.

This makes sense if you are a potential client. Would the same factors attract you if you were commissioning help for others? Yes, because you want them to engage and commit to the process voluntarily rather than being unwilling conscripts. What about if you are a coach? Yes, because working to these principles frees you to be the best of yourself, responsible *to* the client but not *for* the client.

Often when people seek a coach they are ready for a change. If you're feeling stuck, being given access to a coach can also be really good for morale. 'It's great to have been given a coach,' one manager said to us. 'I've been feeling for months that I've hit a kind of glass ceiling – I've been so frustrated.' Often clients sense coaching could have profound implications: 'I've got exactly the same problem in my work, in my relationship with my sons and even with my dog!' said another client. 'I know that if we can get even one of these to shift, the others will, too.'

So what's so special about the way a coach relates to their client? It's a mixture of blame-free realism on the one hand and faith on the other: the realism builds trust, and the faith supports and encourages – a very potent and empowering mixture.

Coaching is blame free but this doesn't mean that it condones or colludes. Coaching aims to truly reflect what *is*, which is sometimes taxing for both coach and client. It is always founded on a deep respect for clients *as they are*, even while seeking to help them realise more of their potential. Coaching helps clients to address what's hard, and to relish – rather than to overlook or discount – what comes easily. Sometimes it can be as hard to accept one's good points, as it is to learn to take criticism as useful feedback: coaching doesn't dodge the need for either. Coaching respects the client's right to choose while at the same time inviting them to consider more options than they did before.

Through the experience of seeing themselves with greater objectivity, clarity – and, often, charity – than usual, the client begins to build a new way of self-monitoring and self-valuing. It is one in which plain truths are not the same as negative judgements, and nurturing self-worth is not the same as being self-deluded or self-satisfied.

A (very) brief history of coaching

In one sense coaching has a very long history indeed. For as long as there have been elders and leaders who provoked insight through deep questioning, the core of coaching could be said to have existed in a variety of cultural and religious traditions around the world. In the Western tradition the most familiar example is probably the Socratic method developed in ancient Greece. Socrates was not interested in imparting information but in questioning what would otherwise be carelessly presupposed: 'I cannot teach anybody anything, I can only make them think.' This was no mere cerebral endeavour. It had a profound existential dimension because, in Socrates' own words, 'the unexamined life is not worth living'.

However, though the essence of coaching is ancient, coaching as we understand it today is a much more recent creation and the coaching profession more recent still. With a young profession it is always perilous to attempt a history. So often it needs the passage of time before we can accurately determine just how influential various contributors have been. Equally, little noticed tributaries often turn out to have been far more significant than first thought. Nevertheless, in what follows we will highlight some of the main elements that are already apparent.

While there have been sports coaches for many, many years it was only in 1975 that Tim Gallwey offered a radical re-evaluation of what really worked in achieving improved performance with *The Inner Game of Tennis*. Rather than exhortation or detailed procedural instructions, Gallwey had found in his own work as a tennis coach that he was most effective when he helped clients attend to their own internal mental processes. In many ways his work enabled clients to get out of their own way. Among Gallwey's students were business people who could see the extraordinary relevance of his approach to the challenges they faced in corporate life. This, combined with favourable television exposure, meant that Gallwey and his newly trained Inner Game coaches were soon spending as much time working in corporations as on the tennis court. One of Gallwey's students, John Whitmore, became closely associated with bringing the Inner Game approach to Europe and in 1995 published *Coaching for Performance*.

In the late 1970s business consultant, philosopher, one-time Chilean cabinet minister and then political prisoner, Fernando Flores settled in California. With Professor Hubert Dreyfus he developed a way of working with language which would form the basis of what has become known as Ontological Coaching. This draws on diverse sources ranging from J.L. Austin to Heidegger. Ontology in this context is concerned with what it is to be human.

In this model language does not just convey information, it is a crucial means whereby we connect and commit to each other. We engage in five kinds of speech acts; we declare, request, assert, offer and promise. So are the ones we're engaging in working for us? Frequently new conversations are needed, especially with clearer requests and promises.

This way of thinking has been developed by Julio Olalla (founder of the Newfield Network), Rafael Echeverria (founder of Newfield Consulting) and James Flaherty (founder of New Ventures West). All worked with Flores at Logonet, his educational company, for years and have been offering coach training for many years now.

Meanwhile traditional sports coaches were also being hired as public speakers by some companies. After all, they were used to inspiring high performance in teams and fostering leadership so maybe there were lessons to be learnt and skills that could be transferred to the corporate world.

By the beginning of the 1990s a number of people were seeking to formalise what they had individually been developing into a more structured and learnable discipline which is today a large part of what we mean when we speak of coaching. In 1992 Thomas Leonard, a former financial planner, founded Coach University. In the same year Laura Whitworth, former Peace Corps Volunteer and CPA along with Henry Kimsey-House founded the Coaches Training Institute. Both organisations have been offering coach training ever since and have now been joined by many other accredited coaching bodies around the world.

In 1998 the members of the Professional Personal Coaches Association and the International Coach Federation came together to form the International Coach Federation with a view to enhancing the standards and standing of coaching. Initially largely North American, the ICF has now become truly international and accredits at a variety of levels. Other bodies such as the European Mentoring and Coaching Council have also been formed which seek to develop standards. However, to date the ICF is far and away the largest non-profit professional association of coaches worldwide with chapters in over thirty countries.

Since the late 1980s there has been an explosion of interest in coaching. The downside of this has been the bandwagon effect: suddenly everybody is 'a coach'. The upside has been the development of numerous credible coaching schools, a drive to establish professional standards, the undertaking of research into the efficacy of coaching, and more recently, business and academic recognition.

It is highly likely that as time passes and coaching approaches are adopted in many different countries we will see more pronounced cultural variations in coaching. Already much European coaching has one interesting component that is more apparent than in its North American counterpart. Many of its practitioners have experience and training in Neuro-Linguistic Programming (NLP). From the mid-1970s and on to the present day NLP has been concerned with two things, seeking models of excellence in any field of human endeavour and understanding the *structure* of our subjective experience. It began by modelling outstanding personal change agents. Successful modelling means it is possible to replicate what works and make it available to anyone who wants to learn. NLP's outcome focus, time-tested techniques and attention to the neuro-linguistics of change have made it naturally attractive for many interested in coaching. The two strands came together explicitly in The European NLP Coaching Programme in 1999. This programme, which has since become the largest indigenous European ICF accredited coach training programme, is provided by International Teaching Seminars.

One of the most striking things about so many of the contributors to the field is their focused approach to change. Whether it was sports performance (Tim Gallwey), financial planning (Thomas Leonard), accounting (Laura Whitworth), or computerised work flow management (Fernando Flores), all were used to focusing – and being assessed – on results. From the outset this orientation has informed the field. While this is not all there is to coaching, it ensures a certain rigour and discipline of approach among fully trained coaches, whether they are addressing performance enhancement with executives or the spiritual aspirations of an individual client.

The supportive mirror

In recent years British television has screened a programme called *What Not to Wear*, which has helped many people to reassess not only the image that their clothing presents, but also the very identity that underlies it. For most 'clients' of the programme, this has been a transforming and liberating experience. As part of the consultation, the client is asked to enter a space where they are entirely surrounded by mirrors, so that they can see themselves from every angle. After a few minutes, the consultants open the mirrored doors, and their faces frame that of their client as they begin the process of helping them to see both what is and what could be.

Coaching, too, provides its own mirror moments. It offers a model for self-evaluation, self-development and self-monitoring, which derives its strength from the use of multiple perspectives in a supportive climate that promotes the client's resourcefulness.

How does coaching work?
Coaching is driven by process not by content

By this we mean that while of course it doesn't ignore content, its primary focus is not narrative (what happened), or detail (who, what, when), or reasons and histories (why), but rather the patterns and issues that underlie the story the client brings. So, while coaching operates at all logical levels (see Chapter 3) it often concerns itself with *how*. For example: how does someone regularly end up feeling they have failed?

How does someone keep choosing the 'wrong' partners? How does someone with the best intentions keep opening their mouth and putting their foot in it? How does someone who is really at ease with clients and subordinates strike his superiors as 'difficult', 'awkward' or 'unsuitable for promotion'? Conversely, how does someone who is comfortable with superiors and peers come across to subordinates as 'distant', 'authoritarian' or 'unapproachable'? How does someone with imagination, sensitivity and talent go on getting 'dead-end' jobs, get stuck in a rut at work or remain in a subservient role as a partner?

Commissioners can find this as much a conundrum as do the clients they manage. Coaching is predicated on the belief, borne out by experience, that if you know *how* you can find out which bits of the recipe to change. As we said in our earlier book *The NLP Coach*, 'failure has a structure'. Therefore it can be understood and doesn't have to be repeated. Conversely, helping someone understand how they have constructed their successes also helps them to replicate them.

Coaching is about involvement and action, about now and the future. It's about knowing what characteristics and qualities are in your personal portfolio, understanding their upsides and downsides, and learning to manage them with more deliberation, targeting and quality control.

Coaching is transparent

Coaching shows you how it works. Even where it gives the 'bottom line' it reveals its mechanisms, so that you can take them on board and use them for yourself. Sometimes a client may take away a rule of thumb that helps them remember what to do, or not do; sometimes the key to unlocking a problem will be more complex, but the tools will have been demonstrated in action and handed over. Of course, coaches have plenty of knowledge and experience – of the processes of change and growth, of the way people structure and make sense of their experience. They will draw on all of these resources, to ask pertinent questions, to help a client discover how they get stuck and how they can get moving again, to find out what they want and to explore what they are capable of. Coaching is *available* magic. Its magic circle welcomes the client in.

Coaching engages the client in self-exploration, self-discovery and self-determination

Coaching assumes that each person is unique, and that only they can find out what works for them. This means that a large part of the coaching process is concerned with engaging the client in self-work, self-discovery and self-transformation in order that any changes are individually tailored to *that* person's needs. Thus even superficially, similar issues can result in quite different solutions with different clients. One newly promoted manager found it difficult to give direction to his staff because they and he had been equals in the same team for a long time. Another experienced a similar difficulty – but this time it was because she couldn't bring herself to set or maintain clear boundaries. Yet another found it hard to manage people who were older than he was and had been in the firm longer. Similar problem, different causes – and so different solutions were needed.

Coaching works by asking not telling

One of the main ways in which a coach engages the client in exploring and discovering is through asking questions. Chapter 7 shows how this works and how the right kinds of questions can initiate significant work at many levels. There's another effect, though. When someone tells you something – their opinion, their diagnosis, their suggestions – you are passive and may perhaps even feel inferior. Think of teachers, experts, doctors and even some kinds of therapists. When someone asks you a question that requires you to search and explore internally, you become the expert instead. You know about you. The message is that your answer matters. It will help shape what happens next. This kind of questioning can be one way in which coaching reinforces your personal identity and worth. It is empowering because it puts you in the driving seat, even if the content of your answers reflects difficulties, weaknesses or problems.

Think about the impact of this, for an individual seeking help at a time of crisis or indecision, say an employee designated as in need of remedial help. Feelings of weakness, inferiority or even resentment tend to melt away in the presence of genuine, respectful enquiry.

Here is an example of how this can work. A senior manager with high-level technical expertise who was told that further promotion depended on him acquiring unfamiliar 'people skills', felt angry that the skills that had served him well so far were now somehow insufficient. He was resentful and inclined to sabotage coaching as something that aimed to 'fix' what didn't need fixing. He arrived late for his first appointment, left his mobile phone on so that he had to break off the discussion to take an 'urgent' call and was 'much too busy' to find time for a second appointment the following week. During that second session his coach alluded to that powerful cocktail of anger, self-doubt and anxiety about having to learn new skills that clients in similar situations had felt. She went on to remind the client that learning new skills often made people feel anxious – but his track record already proved that he could do this when he set his mind to it. This gave him an opening, and he began to explain how he felt that his firm footing was suddenly giving way beneath him. Grudgingly, he admitted that he felt inadequate when confronting feelings rather than targets and charts – but he did want to move up the career ladder and maybe if this was what it took ...

Not all so-called coaches work like this, however. We interviewed a potential client who had 'had coaching' before. (In itself, this phrase probably indicated what the experience felt like: perhaps a dose of something designed to do him good?) When we asked what he had learnt from this experience, he replied, 'I learnt that my childhood had taught me to be a low-maintenance kind of person, and that this was causing some of my problems at work.' What we deduced from this reply was that he had received some kind of therapy, not coaching. Although he had found the insight meaningful, there was no indication that it had been *useful* or that it had enabled him to change himself or his behaviour: the very fact that here he was awaiting a further 'dose' of coaching was evidence of that.

Another kind of telling that's very common in low-grade or pseudo-coaching is offering solutions or advice. 'Why don't you ...?' 'How about ...?' 'I think you should ...' 'What I would do is ...' Again such an approach effectively disempowers the client because it puts the speaker, not the client, in the power seat. Effectively, it says 'You can't manage this on your own.'

This doesn't mean that coaches require their clients to reinvent the wheel. Often, however, a crucial part of adding value comes from what the client is learning through the *process* of being coached. They are learning to seek and build trust in their own experience, to refine their own judgements, to push the boundaries of what they know. They are learning to feel equal in more fundamental and far-reaching ways than can be summed up by finite knowledge and describable skills. They are validating themselves at the level of identity.

Coaching isn't limited by a problem-solving focus

Often, people seek help when they have a problem or experience a deficit. Coaching may begin with a remedial or problem-solving focus, but good coaching always looks beyond this. Why does this matter? Well, fixing a problem is useful – but if you stop there you strictly limit what is possible for yourself and others and you've missed an opportunity. Take the old chestnut, 'Have you stopped beating your wife?' Of course, it's an improvement if the man can say, 'Yes' – but why not go on to learn how to build a harmonious, even an enjoyable and mutually rewarding, relationship with her?

Your goal might be to learn some new parenting skills – but if you're getting on better with your children wouldn't it be worthwhile exploring how those same interpersonal skills could be cascaded into getting on better with your colleagues ... your friends ...?

This two-for-one effect can be an added bonus for the commissioner who has hired a coach on a 'remedial' brief; because of the way good coaching operates its effects almost always reach further than the original issue being targeted. You might hire a coach to help an employee become more confident in their new management role. How much better if they get the opportunity of learning how they can apply their new skills to managing themselves better, too? Wherever you start from, it's always worth maximising your return on the energy you're investing by considering the key coaching question – And what else? What else might this apply to? Where else could I use this? Who else might benefit? Who else could I use this with? And so on. This is the kind of approach that gets you moving along the continuum from remedial towards generative working, and opens up new possibilities. To go beyond a problem focus is to open the doors to a wider, systemic sphere of influence. We explore this theme more fully in Chapter 15.

Coaching is about more than making to-do lists

Coaching can certainly involve plenty of doing, but good coaching goes beyond constructing to-do lists and then ticking them off item by item.

Some 'life-coaches', including those featured in newspapers and magazines, tend to oversimplify and limit what coaching can achieve by overemphasising this kind of straightforward task focus. It certainly sounds, and often feels, purposeful; but unless it goes along with reflecting, exploring and questioning, its immediate attractiveness can lure you into settling for what Ian calls 'the illusion of purposefulness'. By contrast, good coaching investigates and furthers purposefulness at a much deeper level (see Chapter 10).

Coaching assumes discovery and surprise

Unlike teaching, coaching involves more than passing on what's already known. It's not even akin to so-called 'discovery' learning, where the discoveries are sometimes engineered so that the 'right' results are achieved. No, we're talking about genuine discoveries, and genuine surprises. They can take many forms. A client may suddenly achieve a new insight into themselves or their situation. Or they may try out a newly learnt skill in a different situation, and find it works there, too. They might mull over what was discussed in a session – and suddenly find they have moved forwards not one but several steps in their thinking, in their confidence, and in what they feel able to tackle.

One young man who had come to coaching with a very low sense of self-worth astonished both himself and his coach after only a few sessions by going to his boss and asking for a rise. Six months later he had blossomed so much that he was given a whole new project to develop and launch. It was as though the work they had been doing had suddenly begun to achieve not proportional but exponential results. The human resources manager who had commissioned the coaching was both surprised and delighted. 'Coaching this employee delivered far more than any of us had expected,' she said.

How does coaching make this possible? It does so by generating a climate of faith without pressure, of expectancy without specific expectations. The message that the coach gives is consistent. In their behaviour, and not just in their words, they tell the client, 'I accept you as you are now. I salute your discoveries and your achievements without measuring their size or setting a standard you have to live up to. I really wonder what you may be capable of. I look forward to your finding out.'

Coaching harnesses unconscious knowledge, resourcefulness and creativity

Many skill-based forms of helping work largely or exclusively with conscious processing. On the other hand, some forms of helping (such as therapy) emphasise the key role of unconscious processes and may even treat them as impenetrable by non-experts. Coaching works with both forms of mental activity, assuming that each is a necessary – *and accessible* – resource. Questions that invite internal search (see page 87), pauses that give room for reflection and speculation (see page 91), encouragement to notice and monitor (calibrate) changes in physiological states (see page 95) and responses all work towards making the unconscious dimension more open and more available as a resource that the client can draw on.

Coaching makes the assumption that the unconscious is a benign part of the self – and that people can become more conversant with its ways and more fluent in its language. In fact, our own belief in the incredible value of working with every part of the body and mind is such that it led us to write a whole book, *Your Inner Coach*, exploring the value of these intra-personal connections.

The success of coaching is evidenced by the client's actions, not just by what they say

Have you ever been in a situation where someone has asked you whether you enjoyed something, or found it valuable, and you felt obliged to say 'yes'? The great thing about coaching is that it doesn't rely for verification upon loaded evidence like this. The proof of coaching is how the client behaves. It's as simple as that. When someone's behaviour becomes more effective, or confident, or more influential, or more subtle, or less destructive, less tentative, or less indecisive, as they go through coaching, that's real evidence of changes that stem from integrated, repeatable, self-owned learning.

Wendy often works with riders to help them communicate more effectively with their horses. Horses, being prey animals, have highly developed sensitivity to what's happening around them, and reflect in their behaviour much of what's going on in their riders. Thus when a rider is anxious, self-doubting or worried about something, their horse acts as a natural – and sometimes amplifying – mirror. He doesn't understand what the rider is thinking or feeling, of course: he simply reflects what they are unconsciously communicating through their mind–body state. Coaching that helps the rider feel less stressed, and more at ease, focused, purposeful and less afraid, will be visible in the behaviour of the horse – not just in the long term but often right now, this minute. Pretending doesn't cut it with horses. This same evidential basis in changing behaviour is what all good coaching demonstrates.

Coaching is a process that is uniquely placed to help a huge range of people in widely varying contexts with many different issues. It is flexible and ultimately economical because it can deliver a great deal for relatively low investments of time and money. Here's how it does this.

First, it engages you because you get to design the working alliance with your coach. By identifying your own goals and the resources you need to achieve them, you take control and ownership of the process and its results. Next, because it focuses on the practical here and now as well as the bigger picture with its longer-term aims, it ensures that you see the wood – and not just this week's trees. Because its way of working is transparent it means you'll be learning how to coach yourself and others even as you yourself are coached.

And then there's the all-important coaching mindset. More often than not coaches presuppose that people have got what it takes; they assume wholeness not brokenness, resourcefulness and adequacy rather than inadequacy, in their clients. This energises and supports people in taking responsibility and making decisions for themselves and they become more proactive and self-confident. Overall, the outstanding benefit of coaching to all it affects is that people being coached can not only achieve the immediate goals they come with but also, in the process, become more effective at managing themselves.

Chapter Two

MultiModal Coaching

Discovering structures at play is the stock and trade of people with high levels of personal mastery. Sometimes these structures can be readily changed. Sometimes, as with structural conflict, they change only gradually. Then the need is to work more creatively within them while acknowledging their origin, rather than fighting the structures. Either way, once an operating structure is recognised, the structure itself becomes part of 'current reality'. The more my commitment to the truth, the more creative tension comes into play because current reality is seen for what it really is. In the context of creative tension, commitment to the truth becomes a generative force, just as vision becomes a generative force.

Peter M. Senge, *The Fifth Discipline*, Century Business, 1990, page 160

What distinguishes excellent coaching? In our experience, the foundation of all really good coaching is that it is appropriately targeted. Skilful coaches of all persuasions often achieve this naturally, because they monitor the client's communication simultaneously on many levels. But coaching conversations are very complex, and even experienced coaches can sometimes feel adrift. As coach or client, how can you ensure that you are tackling the 'real' issue? How can you then identify the precise intervention that will make the maximum difference with the least expenditure of effort?

Ian's MultiModal coaching model offers you a way to address these questions, to focus productively and to intervene both simply and powerfully. It does this by offering you four fundamental diagnostic tools. These ensure that the goal for any specific coaching work is considered in the round and that you are not leaving out anything important. It enables you to check that proposed changes are not random shots at a distant target but deliberate shifts that will have desirable systemic consequences. Where unexpected results occur, where difficulties and resistances crop up, the model gives you the means of understanding just what has caused them and just where to make further changes. It gives you the keys to a process of ongoing and effective change-making. It enables you to learn from 'failure' and disappointment just as much as from success. It offers you a comprehensive structure and it's a model that seems to fit most people's way of thinking.

The purpose of this chapter is to introduce the MultiModal model as a framework for you to use, whichever role you play in the coaching partnership. We find people really like it whether they are coaches, clients or commissioners of coaching, and that's important because excellent coaching is not determined by the coach alone. In our experience *all* the parties – commissioner, coach and client – are involved in determining its effectiveness.

If you are a commissioner, this model can help you work out what your organisation or your individual staff member needs from a coach, find the right kind of coach and brief them appropriately. If you are a coach it will help you focus your energies and those of your client on the key issues and find the best means of achieving leverage for change. This model, however, isn't only for the coach and the commissioner to use. If you are a client, it enables you to learn more rapidly from your coaching sessions, and to understand just how the work you and your coach are doing is improving your effectiveness. Even more importantly, it becomes a tool you can make your own and use independently both now and in the future. And if you're simply interested in adopting a coaching *approach* in different situations, having these distinctions will be invaluable to doing so easily and effectively.

Good coaching is inclusive, focused and personally transformative. There's a lot to monitor, and a lot to work with. Good commissioners just 'naturally' seem to choose the right coaches. Good coaches just seem to work instinctively – through training and practice their work is 'seamless'. Good clients seem to be quick and diligent learners. But we know there's more to it than that. Behind such words as 'instinctive', 'natural' and 'seamless' lie skills of observation, judgement and enquiry, and many moments of reflection and decision-making. Every commissioner was once a new commissioner; every coach was once a novice; every client was once a newcomer to the process. Becoming effective, effortless and excellent, in every role, involves *learning*.

MultiModal coaching in brief

The MultiModal coaching model is designed to offer you the fruits of that learning process. It will also give you a common language of description, identification and analysis which makes for greater intellectual clarity. Most people find that, once introduced, the terms become a natural part of the way they think about the world and make sense of what's going on.

We want to give you an overview of the four elements of MultiModal coaching before we explore them in detail. This is what they are:

1. Logical Levels

It seems to be natural for people to distinguish between different levels when referring to aspects of their experience. As one of our clients once memorably put it, 'On one level the house burning down was a disaster, but on another level it's what made me the man I am. Because I had to move away I had to start again and that's how I built my own business and I've never looked back.' Our client was aware that the same event – his house burning down – could be considered both as an event (which happened to be a disaster) and as some kind of trigger for a whole new life. What started as an event shook up his sense of who he was and what he wanted from his life. So it had repercussions on quite a different level.

2. The Remedial-Generative Continuum

Are you trying to remedy a problem or generate new possibilities – or both? Problem-solving tends to take us towards the remedial end of the intervention spectrum. Generating new choices and perspectives is very different and belongs more at the generative end of how we might work. Both have their place in coaching and it's important to know which you're going for at any given time.

3. The Systemic Context

'No man is an island,' said John Donne. Every individual is embedded in networks of interpersonal connections which will react to his or her actions; every group, organisation, culture and nation is connected to others, affecting them and being affected by them; every thought has its repercussions in behaviour and physiology. Each of these can constitute a system in its own right. Each also interconnects and affects other systems. Coaching requires us to go beyond immediate observations and choices and become aware of these systemic ramifications. This is also the basis for successful strategic thinking.

4. The Interpersonal-Intra-Psychic Continuum

We have an inner world that often affects how we function in the world at large. Different elements of our psyche can be helping or hindering us. Often we may be able to achieve significant improvements in our interpersonal dealings with others by making sure we're all of a piece inside ourselves first. This is the domain of the intra-psychic. In coaching it's critical to know when to focus on each of these if you want to achieve maximum results.

Each of these four elements is extremely useful in its own right. Together they add up to a pretty comprehensive template for coaching that gives you a remarkably powerful way of making sense of what's going on, how to intervene and where to go next. Working with this straightforward template allows you to ask questions that get right to the heart of what's needed in coaching. For example:

- What kind of issue is at stake? Is it more involved than at first seems apparent? Where is the right place to intervene for change?

- How far is the issue to do with remedying a deficit or weakness, and how far is it about generating new behaviours, new solutions or even new ways of looking at the problem itself?

- Even though the individual is the focus of coaching, how far are their issues or problems shaped by the personal and professional systems in which they operate? What might be the effects on those systems of any changes brought about through coaching?

- How much is the issue to do with the way this person engages with others versus how they engage with themselves?

Logical Levels

The set of distinctions known as Logical Levels can help us identify underlying structures and patterns in our thinking about ideas, events, relationships or organisations. We owe them to the pioneering work of Robert Dilts. (R. Dilts & J. DeLozier, *Encyclopedia of Systemic Neuro-Linguistic Programming*, NLP University Press, Scotts Valley California 2000)

Categorising according to different levels is a way of making important distinctions in our experience. Each of the levels gives us a different kind of information. Often it answers a particular kind of question, and this gives us one way of remembering what the levels are. For clarity, we've put the key question for each level beside it in capitals.

Environment: WHERE? and WHEN?

The level of environment includes obvious things like your surroundings, the external context, the *where* and the *when*. But it also embraces more nebulous elements like your social environment. There is also your internal environment, which you create through your thoughts, feelings and somatic sense of well-being.

Behaviour: WHAT?

Behaviour is *what* you do – or don't do. It involves both deliberate and 'accidental' actions, occurring at both conscious and unconscious levels. Issues on this level relate to what is happening or being done.

Capability: HOW?

Capability is about the *how* and the *how-tos* of life – the knowledge, skills and processes that make it possible for one person who has them to find doing something easy, and for another who lacks them to find the same thing really difficult. These abilities may be inherent or learnt.

Beliefs and values: WHY?

Beliefs and values provide the criteria for judgement and action – the *why* – for both individuals and organisations. Our beliefs and our values shape our understanding of why things are possible or impossible for us. They provide us with a rationale and drive our actions.

Identity: WHO?

Identity is to do with sense of self. This could be our personal identity or a corporate identity – in either case, *who* we are. Psychologically, this area is felt to be most significant and will be most well defended. If someone feels criticised at this level, they will tend to react very strongly!

Beyond identity: FOR WHOM/FOR WHAT?

This is the level that relates to a bigger picture or larger system where questions about some larger purpose come into play. For us as individuals this often means the spiritual. It takes us into questions about our mission. The dimension of mission and vision can also apply to groups and organisations. Because it gives meaning to our life by answering questions about *for whom or for what* larger vision are we working, it can be emotionally supercharged and – as with certain religious groups – heavily defended or aggressively promoted.

The Logical Levels framework gives you a way of understanding:

- What kind of information you are dealing with.

- Where a problem originates.

- On what level the problem is being experienced or manifested – these may not be the same.

- What the 'real' issue at stake is.

- What the appropriate level is for interaction or intervention.

If you are mindful of the key questions – Where/when? What? How? Why? Who? Who or What else? – in any interaction with others, or in relation to your own thinking, you can usually identify the level involved. This in turn enables you to do other important things.

You can find out where a difficulty is really coming from, as opposed to where it seems to originate – for example, problem behaviours often originate in people's beliefs. You can also find out where the points of leverage are to change a situation. People will find it easier to change a behaviour if they can be reassured that it doesn't involve them changing at a belief or identity level.

The Logical Levels framework also enables you to pinpoint small interventions which can bring about larger effects: for example, providing a water cooler or coffee machine in an office (an environmental change) is likely to draw people to it (behaviour), which in turn may help them create or maintain a sense of belonging to a department or team (identity).

Often tone and emphasis make it clear which Logical Level is important. If someone says 'I don't want to go to the *movies*' you might reasonably infer that they would like to *do* something. So you're dealing with behaviour. If, however, they say '*I* don't want to go to the movies' it's not the same message, even though the words are identical. Someone else may well want to but *I* don't. So this is much more at an identity level.

Think of Logical Levels:

- When you or others react to an apparently simple or trivial situation with more feeling than seems to be warranted. Almost certainly there's something going on at the level of belief or identity.

- When you want to make changes in your life, or in an organisation. Consider at which level you are attempting to do this, and whether this is the appropriate level. Often organisations need to win hearts and minds – which means they need to operate at the level of belief and identity. Too often, though, they try a quick fix at the level of behaviour.

- Where there seems to be more involved than is obvious on the surface.

- When offering criticism or praise. Criticism is most easily received if it is pitched at the level of environment or behaviour (and possibly capability), and least effective when delivered at an identity level because we feel a need to defend ourselves if our identity seems under attack. Praise is most effective when offered on higher levels, especially because we take it on board as part of who we are.

In coaching the levels can be used to identify what the real issues are. They can help you find the simplest or most effective point for leverage. Use them to help in rapport building, by respecting what may be involved for yourself or others at an unconscious level. Use them to help you understand situations that seem puzzling: just what is the issue here, and what Logical Level is it at? Use them to help you assess 'fit' – between people and jobs, between people and environments, and between problems and proposed solutions.

While the levels are often regarded and set out as a hierarchy – frequently shown as a ladder with *beyond identity* at the top or, alternatively, as a set of concentric circles with *beyond identity* at the centre – this does not imply a hierarchy of importance in terms of value, any more than the roots of a tree are more important than its leaves. A tree needs both – and all the structures in between. When you are working with trees, you need to know which part you are dealing with: the same is true for individuals and organisations.

Working with this tool enables you to ask yourself several key questions about any coaching issue or need:

- On which level is the immediate issue/symptom occurring?

- What other levels may be involved? Is the problem actually being generated at a different level, as in the case of the manager we'll describe later (see page 40), whose intransigent behaviour was actually defending his identity?

- What is the most appropriate level on which to take action? Sometimes a change at a lower level may bring about corresponding change at higher levels – as, for example, when installing that water cooler. This simple environmental change fosters people chatting at the watering hole, which is part of how people build and nurture networks and feel they belong. Conversely, lower-level changes can sometimes happen more easily as a result of higher-level changes, as with an adolescent we coached, whose behaviour improved once she developed a greater and more independent sense of her own worth.

The Remedial-Generative Continuum

Coaches are often approached for help in setting something right that is perceived as inadequate, lacking or wrong. In these circumstances, the drive for coaching is essentially corrective: set me straight, help us out, and fix it!

We would like you to think of coaching in less restrictive terms – as a process that certainly has direction, but that doesn't have to be based on righting errors. To get the most out of coaching think of it as taking place on a continuum that has remedial coaching at one end and generative coaching at the other.

remedial<—————————————————————————>*generative*

What do we mean by this and what are the implications for commissioning and co-experiencing coaching when you approach it in this way?

Many people who have experienced excellence in coaching tell us that it has gone beyond what they expected. It has helped them find solutions that were quite new or radical, and it has changed the very thinking that held the original 'problem' in place; it has changed *them*. (Notice this takes the change to the level of identity.) This can happen even when the commissioning brief is a remedial one. When you enquire more closely you find that somehow the process did rather more than just fix a problem; it gave rise to some new thinking; it stimulated creativity; it generated multiple options. When you 'think outside the box' you do much more than right what was originally wrong or supplement a deficiency or just catch up. You find new pathways, see new terrain, gain a new perspective and sometimes find a better place to go to.

Much of our thinking in business, in education and in daily life is predicated on problem-solving. The problem effectively defines the solution in its own terms. Poor sales need to get better. Unproductive workers have to become more productive. Debilitating relationships should become more tolerable. But as Einstein commented, no problem can truly be solved with the same kind of thinking that created it. We need new terms, fresh approaches, and different ways of *thinking*.

Even just placing a coaching brief on the remedial–generative continuum gives us a different stance in relation to it. By asking 'just how remedial?' or 'just how generative', we are beginning a process of exploration; and we are acknowledging that no problem is entirely remedial – or entirely generative. When we achieve a more effective form of behaviour, or improve our environment, or enhance or learn a skill, our thinking and our self-esteem are likely to improve. This is generative when it triggers behaviours, thoughts, actions and feelings that were not possible before. When one individual who is in a position of influence within a social or work context changes for the better, they change the context they provide for the others around them. And this, of course, can be very generative.

Really good coaching can hardly avoid being generative because the coach always models reflection, enquiry and the habit of self-monitoring to the client through their own approach to the interaction.

- **Reflecting** When you reflect, you take time to stand back from your immediate situation. You change your experience. You gain a whole new perspective. This tends to disrupt mindless habitual responses that are not working for you.

- **Enquiring** When you answer a thoughtful or probing question – one which your coach asks knowing its importance but without knowing the answer – it is hard to repeat a well-rehearsed or stock rationalisation. Powerful questions delve deeper and get you searching in new directions.

- **Self-monitoring** As you become self-monitoring you develop a new way of being with yourself. You begin to feel that you know what's going on inside yourself more, which means you feel more in control. You're also able to tap into your own intuition much more easily and often. Even clients who already reflect, already enquire and already self-monitor find that coaching enhances both the extent and the effectiveness of these processes.

Where coaching addresses a specific deficiency and helps the client make needed improvements, it rightly and valuably meets a remedial need. If, however, all three parties to the interaction recognise that even remedial work can have far-reaching implications, acknowledge them and perhaps take time to explore what they might be, then far greater benefits can be achieved.

The labels 'remedial' and 'generative' point to a mindset that can have a profound effect on the process of coaching and the kind of value it can deliver. Some commissioners have a remedial mindset. So do some coaches – and some clients. This tends to limit what they could do and what they can achieve.

The converse is also true. Some commissioners 'just seem to' select the best coaches; some coaches 'just seem to' get results, and some clients 'just seem to' get a lot out of their coaching. There is no 'just seem to' about it. Your mindset determines what you presuppose about the possible outcomes of coaching (your beliefs). What you believe and value will affect what skills you choose to develop and how you exercise them (your capabilities). These skills will affect how you are able to act (your behaviour). And your behaviour will affect your sense of self (your identity).

The Systemic Context

The essence of mastering systems thinking ... lies in seeing patterns where others see only events and forces to react to.

Peter M. Senge, *The Fifth Discipline,Century Business*, 1990, page 126

An awareness of connections and implications is one important strand of a systemic approach. Coaching can help you become alert to the effects you are having and could have on your internal, as well as external, systems. For example, working hard and long is a habit embedded within many individuals and many organisations – a value that drives behaviour which can seem productive but often has negative consequences. Days that are filled with unbroken desk work, with hours staring at computer screens, or that are packed with continuous meetings, take no account of our natural ultradian cycles of activity and rest, (*what rest?*), of our body's need to move and stretch, or even of its regular promptings for nourishment (*lunch? – had a twelve-o'clock then a one-o'clock*). What we label stress is frequently the systemic effect of habits like these.

When we employ a systemic awareness in our coaching we become aware of another key factor: any system is more than the sum of its constituent parts – and it is often this nebulous entity that we most need to take into account. A person is more than the cells and physical systems that comprise them; an institution is more than its employees and physical equipment. Individuals and organisations, families and cultures, all have their distinguishing characteristics and habits – things that are part of them yet go beyond specific constituents. Water consists of molecules of hydrogen and oxygen: its wetness is an *emergent* property not an inherent one. The kindness of one individual, the cohesiveness of a team, the crushingly ambitious drive of an organisation are similarly all emergent properties. Coaching partnerships that can recognise and take account of emergent properties are much more effective.

The systemic approach gives us another important marker: the concept of feedback. Too often in colloquial English 'feedback' is taken to mean comment or evaluation – and frequently this is assumed to be negative. We shall be using the word very differently, though.

When you engage in action it has results or consequences. These can be seen as feedback about what effect you're having. Such feedback is a vital tool in effective coaching, whether you are the coach or the client. One crucial implication of regarding 'results' or 'consequences' as feedback is that feedback is just information – *not success or failure*. 'Failure' can be crushing. 'Success' can be blinding. Both can be overwhelming. 'Feedback' is different. Feedback is what happens as a result of your thinking and your actions. Its value is neutral. It has a high signal value because it carries lots of information if we just pay attention.

In systems thinking feedback does not refer to specific content at all. It is a value neutral term and is a description of dynamic structure – hence the familiar systems term 'feedback *loops*'. Feedback is the defining characteristic of a system – no feedback, no system. We can usefully distinguish between *reinforcing feedback* – more of the same – or *balancing feedback* – something different happening.

We heard of a client with serious personal financial issues whose behaviour was triggering a spiralling reinforcing feedback loop: every month he would max out his credit cards, then open a new one to pay off the minimum deposit required on each of the others! As you can imagine this couldn't go on forever, and that's where the balancing feedback loop kicked in – in his case in the form of the bailiffs coming through the front door and the refusal of further credit.

A systemic approach offers us the opportunity to get outside the box and stop thinking of feedback as just a linear process. Anyone who has really paid attention to how human beings interact will know there is an extraordinary circularity to the way they interact and affect each other. We can even chart how elements affect each other by using feedback loop diagrams.

When people seek to make changes they very often fail to take account of the time it will take for their actions to have an effect. In expecting palpable results too quickly, they may be disappointed. They may then feel the need to repeat or redouble their efforts. Imagine adjusting the steering of a liner. You alter the position of the wheel or rudder: nothing seems to happen. So you alter it even more. By failing to wait you are likely to find that you have made a much greater course correction than you wanted. Anyone who has grappled with unfamiliar hotel shower control settings will know what we mean. First it's too hot, then, after you adjust the setting, it's freezing. In both cases you might feel that there was only delayed feedback. Actually, you just didn't have a way of calibrating to the very subtle changes which you had most definitely set in motion.

Good coaching has evidence procedures agreed between the coach, client and commissioner that are built into the process so everyone can know whether and when they are on course. Systems thinking helps put these in the larger context and gives us a more profound understanding of how the elements comprising the system interact. The pay-off is much greater leverage – and that means faster, easier and more elegant change.

For a thorough introduction to the practical applications of systems thinking see *The Art of Systems Thinking* (see Bibliography, page 186).

Working Interpersonally and Intra-psychically

However astute the commissioner, however committed the client, however skilled the coach, their work will only be effective if it is focused on the right issues. For example, it can be easy to assume that a problem within a partnership is 'either hers or mine'; the issue for a team may appear to be 'leadership', or 'motivation' or 'better communication'; but to take these flags as a signal that coaching should focus on interpersonal work is to miss one crucial possibility: that it may be better targeted on what is occurring *within* the client rather than on what is going on *between* him and others.

The reality we experience is within ourselves just as much as around us. We have conversations with ourselves; we repeat old patterns and relive old experiences; we apply old learning and are governed by learnt expectations. Sometimes this can be helpful; but at other times it means that we are busy making others play to our scripts and hearing them speak the dialogue we know best. We can even cast them as key figures from our past, hanging inappropriate costumes upon them on the strength of a few key similarities.

This is normal, if ineffective. Learning to hold more productive conversations with ourselves, to manage our familiar internal inclinations and attributes, together with those internalised influential people we carry around with us, is an ongoing task of self-management.

For coaching to be truly outstanding, it needs to take account of this dimension. Sometimes it may be obvious even from the outset that work needs to focus on what is going on within the client. At other times, a responsive client or experienced coach will become aware that the real nub of a problem lies here rather than in improving how they interact with others. If you begin by knowing how vital a dimension this can be, you will be more vigilant in looking out for smaller indications and more quickly able to respond to them. Your work will be more elegant, more seamless – and much more effective. For however committed you are and however able your interpersonal skills, they will not be effective in the long term if the real issues lie elsewhere.

MultiModal coaching in action

Bill was a senior manager whose outstanding technical expertise was invaluable to his company but whose people skills seemed decidedly sketchy. Eighteen months ago his annual review had produced strikingly polarised feedback. Some colleagues rated him highly and liked him personally, while others found him unapproachable, dominating and even intimidating. What was going on? The organisation had responded by seeking more evidence, but interviewing more of his colleagues just provided more of the same polarised information.

What did emerge was that most of the concerns were about his manner and his behaviour rather than about his skills or his personal commitment to the work of the organisation. Then the remedy had seemed simple: coaching would help him adjust his behaviour so as to become more accessible, take more account of others and cultivate a less intimidating manner. In fact, this had been tried. But we were hired because nothing had really changed. Why not?

Using the MultiModal template to explore further, we found that Bill hadn't actually changed his view of other people: he still inwardly wrote off many of his peers and subordinates as being ineffective or even 'stupid'. So his behavioural attempts to change how he related to them came across as cosmetic and unreal. Previous coaching had been ineffectual because it was conducted at the wrong Logical Level – that of *behaviour*. He hadn't changed his *beliefs* – and what underlay this was a long-term intra-psychic habit: judging others adversely helped him maintain his own fragile confidence because the more he put them down in his head the more able and intelligent he felt by comparison.

We had been asked to find out what was really going on and then to help Bill improve his performance – a remedial brief. But in order to help him make real and lasting changes we needed to help him generate greater confidence in himself (*identity*) and a better understanding of others. Only through a generative focus could we produce the change desired.

Nor would this be happening in a vacuum. We needed to consider what, if any, contribution the system he was part of made to the problem. As a leader in its field, the organisation he worked for hired outstanding people and pressured its managers to perform through a culture of competitive excellence. However, because it assumed excellence – 'you wouldn't be here if you weren't the best' – the feedback given to staff tended to focus on where they fell short rather than on what they did well. This culture of non-recognition dovetailed all too well with Bill's personal history of critical ambitious parents.

Bill was clear that he would like to feel better about himself and that he was far more critical of himself than he was of anyone else. One early coaching assignment we set was that he was to notice what he was doing that was working and to build on it. This required him to pay attention in a new way. Rather than fixating on what he could have done better, his task was to track his successes, own his accomplishments and report them to his coach.

Equally important was redefining the concept of feedback. Up until now feedback had been offered to Bill about what he needed to improve on or had failed to deliver. We offered Bill a systemic way of thinking about feedback: that his words and actions would be creating reinforcing or balancing feedback loops for good or ill, so he should decide what he thought was most desirable and then act. We encouraged him to give fuller, more specific and more immediate feedback to his people.

Bill decided to institute regular monthly meetings with his direct reports to give them feedback on how they were doing. In this way he shifted the emphasis from a judgemental annual formal evaluation (so much of which he said was 'about the past') to ongoing monitoring and self-monitoring, which involved and empowered them. Because this had such a noticeable effect on raising staff morale, he eventually plucked up the courage to ask his section head, James, to do the same for him. Somewhat surprised, James agreed. Six months later, James extended the pattern of relatively informal monthly reviews to all his direct reports, and asked them to cascade the pattern downwards to include in turn the people they managed.

So what was going on here? The work we had begun on a largely remedial brief had begun to take a more generative direction. It had helped our client realise that some of his interpersonal difficulties were the outward reflection of what was going on intra-psychically. Because he was beginning to address the real issues at an *identity* level, he started to come across differently: he began to approach his staff with a more open and less dismissive attitude (*beliefs and values*), and felt more able to make genuine changes in his *behaviour* towards them. He told us how he now thought the organisation was paying a high price because its culture restricted people's willingness to experiment and to be 'wrong'. By instituting individual monthly meetings he found a way to erode this gradually and non-confrontationally. The turn-around this produced empowered him and gave him the courage to manage upwards in a new way, and this in turn began to impact the organisational culture through the agency of his section head.

How long will it take?

Coaching is itself an incremental process, and is often concerned with furthering other incremental processes. How long will it take to help a client overcome a problem; become more self-aware; acquire greater effectiveness and subtlety in self-management? It all depends on the individual, of course. Questions like these will often arise and will be discussed and agreed as part of designing the alliance (see chapter 4). To avoid any uncertainty one common practice is to agree a set number of sessions. In the final one, progress can be reviewed and a new contract agreed.

Issues at higher Logical Levels may take more to explore and address than those involving the lower levels; remedial work doesn't necessarily have to be completely 'fixed' for the client, the commissioner or the coach to be satisfied that improvements have been made and are likely to continue; interventions that have been thought through in systemic terms will take as long to 'work through' as the slowest speed at which the system itself learns and changes – which is the speed of its slowest component.

Adopting a MultiModal approach

This comes naturally once the distinctions are familiar to you. Getting familiar with the four fundamental distinctions is best achieved by using them. You could do this through the following three exercises, which will put the distinctions to work for you.

▶ **Exercise 1** Next time you are taking a less active part in a meeting, or listening to a conversation between others or hearing an interview on radio or television, ask yourself what is the key Logical Level involved in the discussion.

▶ **Exercise 2** When you are next seeking a solution to a problem, take a few minutes to consider whether the brief is remedial or generative. Could you find additional or better solutions by taking a generative approach? Even where the immediate problem can be fixed by taking remedial action, would a generative approach at another level (for example, considering what contributed to causing the problem in the first place) allow you to use a systemic understanding and generate more far-reaching and beneficial changes?

▶ **Exercise 3** Take a recent event – at work or at home – that has puzzled you, and re-examine it using the MultiModal model. Ask yourself what Logical Level(s) seem to be involved? Was any action you took, or are thinking of taking, predominantly remedial or predominantly generative? What kind of feedback was this event giving you – and how did you interpret it and act on it? What chains of repercussions were/might be set off? What kind of feedback loops do you notice? Were they reinforcing or balancing? Any emergent properties? What intra-psychic or interpersonal elements were involved?

Chapter Three

The Core of Coaching

A Thinking Environment is the set of conditions under which people can think for themselves and think well together. They make it possible for people's thinking to move further, go faster, plumb insights, banish blocks and produce brand-new, exactly needed ideas in record time . . .

We can provide a Thinking Environment for each other anywhere, at any time. But first we have to decide to take the leap. We have to be willing to think for ourselves.

Nancy Kline, *Time to Think: listening to ignite the human mind,*
Ward Lock, 1999, page 27

G ood coaches come with different backgrounds, different theoretical frameworks and many unique combinations of qualities and personality. Coaching can also focus on many different issues, experienced in a variety of different contexts – hence the distinction between 'executive coaching', which describes work that is aimed at helping people become more effective in their business or organisational roles, and 'life coaching', which addresses life issues such as parenting, relationships and self-fulfilment. However, these distinctions are really much less significant than they sound. When you really look at it, all coaching is aimed at helping people manage themselves more effectively. The difference is one of content and context, not one of *process.*

All good coaching, both formal and informal, shares certain core features. As a commissioner deciding whom to employ, as a client choosing the best person to work with, as a coach monitoring what you do and seeking to do it even better, there are four key issues to keep in mind: presence, attention, communication, and self-reflexiveness.

Between them, these are your means of ensuring that any coaching you are involved in has heart and soul. Where any of these elements is limited or lacking, coaching will suffer.

Presence and attention

Check how many of the following have happened to you. While you're talking you suddenly realise that the other person is no longer 'with you'. You're having a professional consultation and it's interrupted by a phone call, or someone knocking on the door, which leaves you hanging and deprives you of your rightful place at the centre of attention. You hear the telltale clicking of that computer keyboard when you're speaking to someone on the phone. How did these behaviours impact you? When we've asked people this they've spoken of a whole range of feelings, from neglected, irritated and put down, through to angry and abandoned to even inferior and worthless.

Good coaching has the opposite effect. The coach contracts to give the client their full attention. They will be *present*, whether the interaction is face to face or via the telephone. Presence transcends role. In many settings professional expertise is often used as a defensive veneer. But for a coach to be present they need to be present as a human being. So in addition to being skilled they need to be prepared to be 'only human': trying to be the best coach you can be doesn't mean pretending or trying to be infallible. It means that you are prepared to experience and show feeling where it's appropriate; that you are prepared to say you don't know, or you're wrong; that you are willing to learn; that you take the risk of being open to different opinions, to unfamiliar ideas, rather than defending your status – or the status quo. It means that you are willing to be uncertain and to experiment. It means recognising when something makes you uncomfortable, and taking the risk of saying so. Or taking the risk of laughing – at the situation and at yourself.

Presence implies all of these things because it's about being *real*. It's about being available. Presence is active and engaged. The most successful coaching occurs when both coach and client can be present in this way. It doesn't justify a coach in indulging in 'me too' anecdotes, or a client in self-pity. But it's the opposite of impersonal expertise, or passive waiting to be helped or treated. Presence communicates active acknowledgement of the other at an identity level.

By contrast, Sara, a friend of ours, had an outpatients' appointment for a scan. A nurse performed the scan, while the consultant dictated his observations into a machine. While diagnosing he used a number of technical terms, and referred to Sara as 'an interesting medical case'. When he had finished, she asked him to explain what some of the terms meant. 'Be thankful that I'm allowing you to listen,' he said. He was attending to the case – but not to the person. Although professionally competent, he was not present.

How is attention different from presence? In our view, it means noticing, listening and remembering. If you're the commissioner or the coach, it means being able to register the actual words and phrases the client uses to describe her experience, rather than referring back to them or redescribing them in *your* words. It means remembering them over time and picking up patterns and their possible underlying meanings, so that the client doesn't have to repeat information she has given you in earlier sessions. Attention is about noting who and how the client is, and unobtrusively letting her know this. It's also about acknowledging that she is a unique individual, and through your behaviour conveying to her that she matters.

Attention is about noticing and making connections – between something that occurs on one Logical Level and its repercussions on other levels. Sometimes it may be appropriate to share what you have noticed; sometimes it is enough to 'log' it – perhaps for future reference, to await more evidence, or to share at a more appropriate time.

How do you show attention if you're the client? You'll be listening, and registering and remembering – not just what others may say to you but, just as importantly, what you are saying to yourself. You'll be learning how to stay in the moment rather than escaping back to the past or into the future, because the present moment is where you have options and choices, even if you make them with reference to what happened before and what may happen in the future. Paying yourself attention in this respectful and thorough way is one of the key tools that enables you both to help yourself now and to learn how to carry on coaching yourself in the future.

Attention above all is about learning to suspend your assumptions. You can't get by in life without them, because assumptions are essentially rules of thumb or conclusions based on experience, and as such they save you constantly reinventing the wheel. But to the extent that you use them unthinkingly to provide templates for thought and action, they can stop you noticing what's really happening. Attention to what *is*, is the best means we have of reality checking what we expect, what we believe and what we fear. It helps us to recognise and deconstruct our own prejudices; it helps us be open to new learning and it helps us make cleaner connections with each other.

So what happens when presence and attention are both lacking? Wendy's husband Leo is a New Zealander. When he took her to New Zealand for the first time he wanted to reconnect with old friends and introduce her to people who had been important to him. One day they went to meet up with his former education tutor and a number of academic colleagues. One of them asked Wendy what work she did then. 'I'm a lecturer in education,' she said. He was too. 'That's interesting,' he said – and passed straight on to something else. Was he present? Had he attended? Presence and attention are the opposite of going through the motions and running on automatic.

Communication

Communication is not just about the words, though coaching works with and through words. Learning to understand each other's language is a beginning. Later, creating and talking a shared language is part of the duet that coach and client create together. The flow of words depends on rapport and trust, both of which are built at many levels. It's striking how many coaches we've heard talk of coaching as a duet or a dance. Both analogies suggest rhythm and reciprocity as central to success. How would it be to think of your next coaching session like this?

Coaching works in the space between and within people, helping them to examine, understand and refashion the understandings of themselves and the world upon which they base their actions within it. The psychoanalyst D.W. Winnicott described play like this, as a form of personal exploration, experimentation and meaning that was often joyous and inherently profound. Coaches – and good commissioners of coaching – let clients know that this space exists, that it is safe and that is *theirs*. They do this through their words, through their facial expressions and body language, and through the way they behave. (More on the how-tos in Section 2.)

As a client, communicating begins with yourself. With an understanding you have with yourself that this process is worth your energy, your exploration, your enquiry and your honest commitment. This is what you'll find yourself communicating to your commissioner and to your coach, through the way you first enquire about coaching, the way you begin to define and articulate your goals for it, and the way you negotiate and design your coaching alliance, even before you get on to the content you want to work on.

Communication happens as much within the client as between the client and those outside them. It happens inside the coach and commissioner, too, as they pay attention to the kind of inner signals and gut feelings that suggest, for example, that *this* client would be best matched with *that* coach; that this issue is a suitable place to begin, while this other, underlying issue may be the one that is really justifying the process; or that now is the moment to make a suggestion, offer an intuition, ask a powerful question ...

Self-reflexiveness

At the very heart of coaching is the ability to see yourself from other perspectives. Sometimes it's about recognising how you may be impacting another person. Sometimes it's about assuming for a moment a helicopter view and surveying the situation – you being part of it – as a whole. Sometimes it's about having an intimate conversation with yourself about how you are, what you think, how you feel and what you want.

Reflection can have far-reaching effects. For example, one senior manager we worked with derived much of his reputation, and hence not just reinforcement of his skills (capabilities) but also an important part of his sense of self (identity), from working hard and delivering what was required. In practice, this often meant that he was rushing from meeting to meeting, fielding incessant phone calls, and sometimes intimidating his colleagues in the process.

Very early on in our work with him, we discussed some possible implications of this driven approach for himself and for those around him, and he began to wonder just how essential – or effective – it was to maintain it at all times. He started to look at himself and his situation from outside.

The third time we met he told us what a difference this reflection was already making. 'I had to go to Brussels last week,' he said. 'Usually I would work a full day here then get the last Eurostar train, arriving in my hotel after midnight and getting up at 6 a.m. the next day as usual. This time I decided to leave here after lunch, get an earlier train and arrive in time for a leisurely supper. My wife and my secretary were both astounded!' 'What effects did you notice?' we asked. 'I was more relaxed and much fresher for the important meetings I had the next day. When I first made the decision I felt rather self-indulgent – but actually it paid off, not just for me but also for what it delivered in business terms. So I shall do the same when I go back again next week.'

The ability to develop this interactive kind of relationship with ourselves is uniquely human – and uniquely beneficial in helping us relate better to others and to ourselves. It's an essential step in developing and maintaining your personal integrity. It helps you know when to be assertive, and when to compromise or give way gracefully – for decisions like this rest on knowing what is really important to you, to the other person and to the situation. It helps you work out why something matters as much as it does – and whether it should. It also stops you opening your mouth and putting your foot in it.

Coaching rests on fostering a self-reflexive awareness. Gradually this becomes a regular part of your life. Even if it's already a habit with you, coaching hones this skill.

SECTION 2: The Nuts and Bolts of Coaching

Overview: Making Each Intervention Tell

> *The present is so rich because so much is happening in it. Most people can't see, feel, or experience it, so they can't benefit from it. If, on the other hand, you actually can see, feel, or experience it, that skill is lever-ageable.*
>
> *By this I mean that you can do more with the present than you can with the past or the future. The present is like yeast, or like a pulley or a fulcrum – anyone who is aware of, and sensitized to, all that is occurring in the present will find that they can do a lot with it.*

Thomas J. Leonard, The Portable Coach, Scribner, 1998, page 256

An intervention is something that, literally, 'comes between' – between an idea and its realisation, or between the beginning of a journey and its eventual destination. Interventions are *active and relate to a desired end*. In coaching any of the parties can intervene – and all do at one time or another. Between them, they steer this co-creation of theirs, the coaching process, in the way it needs to go.

How does this come about, and just what's involved? The process of intervening begins right at the start of coaching. Each chapter in this nuts and bolts section introduces you to a particular kind of intervention – all of these have emerged as characteristic features of excellent practice.

What intervention involves

Even when you have experience of coaching and are being coached, there are moments when you marvel at the skills involved at the very same time as you are experiencing them. You feel a sense of freedom and autonomy, yet you realise this is no accident, and no 'natural growth' either. The experience is being crafted in a mutual dance, in which nothing is superfluous and nothing is wasted. This doesn't mean following a preordained structure: rather, it involves a constant monitoring in the moment, which allows the coaching partners to be selective as they go along about what they say and don't say, which things they pick up and explore further, or which they 'mark' for future reference while apparently ignoring them for the moment. Coaching, in other words, is all about decisions, some of them conscious but many of them arising intuitively through processing outside of conscious awareness.

How can you develop something of this ease? In our experience focusing on four key elements can help you make your interventions really tell. You could ask yourself:

1. What do I target?

2. What's going on here?

3. Does it all hang together?

4. What are the probable knock-on effects?

What can we achieve if we are mindful of these questions? Think of making a journey. If you have a pretty clear idea of where you are going, or what you are looking for or what kind of experiences you would like along the way, you are much more likely to find ways to succeed in your aims. It's the same with coaching. This doesn't mean that you can't change direction, discover new avenues or take time out to explore the unexpected. What it does mean, though, is that your actions are not random but purposeful. This is what makes them worthy of the label 'interventions'. Think of our four questions as ways to prompt you in the right direction.

1. What do I target?

How does a coach know where to target his work? First and foremost, good coaches have developed the ability to monitor what is happening at many levels simultaneously. As a client, you can learn to do this too. While this is a skill that can be learnt and honed, even young children possess its basic elements: they notice everything and ask questions about most things. Think about visiting somewhere new: your eyes are open, and you are constantly alert to what seems familiar and what is strange. You want to understand why. And you may also be wondering how it is to live a life like this. If you add to this a willingness to hold your own values in suspension while you wonder, you are beginning to think like a coach.

If you can do this as a client – at first perhaps momentarily, then more extensively – you are learning to self-coach. You will be looking out for patterns: key concerns, repeated patterns of behaviour, favourite phrases and underlying beliefs, and assessing just how these may be pointers to problems, potential resources or active limitations. For example, a colleague of ours who is a life coach was asked to help a client decide whether to take a promotion she'd been offered. She was very good at her current project-focused work, but had reached a ceiling. The promotion would involve her in less hands-on work and more in people management. Despite the client's outstanding track record and confident manner, the coach noticed words like 'nervous' and 'anxious' cropping up whenever she referred to her possible new role. Pointing this out took the session into a new and really useful area for the client and helped her, in the end, to decide not to take the promotion. 'I'd rather be good at what I know than struggle to make myself what I'm not,' she said.

Some patterns will emerge actively, while others will become apparent because they are *not* mentioned, do *not* occur. For example, in many successful companies people can get so used to being effective that they take good work, able employees and business successes for granted. As a coach, you may begin to notice that some of your clients don't praise others – or recognise themselves. They may be experiencing and reinforcing an emergent property of the system itself: a culture of non-recognition. Logging the way in which certain things are taken for granted can be a first step towards helping your clients surface them, examine their effects and make choices about whether they want or need to make changes.

Coaching, of course, doesn't just involve words. Body language may underscore or at times contradict the overt agenda, and either coach or client can draw attention to this and suggest exploring its significance. As coaching progresses, clients learn to become self-monitoring, and often notice and comment on their changing reactions during a session. 'It's odd, but I feel uncomfortable in saying that.' 'I'm getting hot under the collar just thinking about that.' 'I feel as though every time you mention him I shy away from looking at how I feel when I have to work with him.' Where initially the coach may invite the client to explore further, clients increasingly learn to prompt and orchestrate their own explorations.

2. What's going on here?

When you ask yourself this question, you are for a moment stepping outside your own immediate experience to reflect on it. You are becoming an observer, and you are seeking for information that goes beyond mere events to what underlies them. You are looking for patterns. You may do this by taking 'the helicopter view', or by considering how the same situation is being experienced by different participants. Sometimes these are highlighted by discrepancies, for example, between words and body language, between the apparent importance of what's going on and the degree of feeling it's generating.

This ability to shift your stance with regard to yourself, within coaching and within many other situations, can give you the benefit of 'time out' and of other ways of experiencing and interpreting what is going on. Such differences can help you intervene more accurately in the present and formulate alternative or additional strategies for managing the future. 'What's going on here?' can be a really useful question whichever role you are in, whether you are asking it of your partner or of yourself. It immediately takes you into a higher level of observation and analysis than that afforded by your immediate, here-and-now experience.

3. Does it all hang together?

When coaching works, one reason that it does so is because nothing significant has been left out. This doesn't mean that the partners have gone into exhaustive detail about everything that could possibly be involved, but experienced coaches and committed clients respect anything that doesn't seem to 'fit', and don't override feelings of doubt or indecision. Even when it is tightly focused, coaching respects that it is working with the person as a whole, not just the work problem or life decision that has brought them there. This is where the Logical Levels and the systemic approach can both help: they are tools that help you ensure that you are not just moving one piece of a jigsaw about but rather engaging in a dynamic modification of the whole, like the whole-picture reconfiguration made with a kaleidoscope.

Coaching that respects the whole tends to work with the whole: coaching that works with the whole tends to achieve more effective and lasting results.

As you begin to work within this dimension, keep checking for discrepancies and inconsistencies. They are your pointers to work that still needs doing – valuable feedback, not failure.

4. What are the probable knock-on effects?

Coaching always needs to take account of more than the immediate situation. One man we knew was inspired by his coaching to make radical changes to his work-life balance: for a long time he had felt that he hadn't spent enough time with his wife and family. When he went home and told his wife he had booked a week's holiday on their own and arranged for his parents to mind the children, he was very surprised by her reaction. He expected her to be delighted, but instead she exploded because she had not been consulted, and was then by turns angry and sullen for the next few days. He and his coach had focused solely on his needs, so he had not imagined how his wife might feel, or formulated any strategies for broaching the topic with her. One step forwards in this non-systemic way meant at least two steps backwards before harmony could be restored and a proper discussion begun at home.

Effective coaching addresses a really important question in this area, namely, what is the function of the status quo? Even where apparently dysfunctional or destructive patterns are involved, it is useful to assume that they serve some purpose, which either is currently, or once was, valid. Attempts at change that don't take the status quo into account often come unstuck. One young woman sought coaching because her manager was offering her promotion. 'This always happens,' she said. 'In the past I've gone along with it, but though I'm good at my job, when I've let them promote me in the past I've always regretted it. Each time I think it's a good idea, and I try really hard – until I'm so stressed by the added responsibility that I have to leave. Now I want to get this sorted properly!'

The importance of the four questions

These four questions can help you keep on track, whether you are arranging and monitoring coaching as a commissioner, practising it as a coach or actively working as a client. In addition, there are some particular times when it can be especially worthwhile to use them:

- When you are wondering whether to change direction or elaborate something already said.

- When you feel there's a choice about what to say, or focus on, next.

- When there's a pause: ask yourself if it would be useful to let it continue (see utilising the power of silence, pages 91–92), or if it's time to sum up or change direction.

- When you're the coach and you are tempted to elaborate, to teach or to give advice.

Be guided in such moments by two key principles: good targeting and restraint. As a coach, how do you know you have found the right target? If you ask the wrong question or offer an incorrect interpretation, people will, generally, agree half-heartedly, ignore what you have said – or tell you that you are wrong. If you have found the right target, their reaction will tell you, either in words or in their body language. (Chapters 6 and 7 talk you through some key targeting approaches in more detail.) As a client, you can be guided by your own responses: those 'aha!' moments that tell you something important has been said, or felt – and, on the other hand, that sense of doubt or plain wrongness you get when something just doesn't fit.

If you are the client, you have a choice every time a session is in the offing. What are you going to talk about? If you believe that coaching focuses on problems and deficiencies, you will be expecting to target these. If you have been told by someone else that you 'need coaching', you may be less likely to ask your coach for help in working out what you really want from your life. To a large extent, you will sort out such major framing questions as you and your coach design your working alliance; but the decisions you make before every session about where to start can really help you get the most out of your coaching.

In coaching as in other fields, less is usually more. This means giving yourself and your partner time to think, to explore and to be tentative, rather than keeping a verbal back and forth going or only opening your mouth when you are sure you can articulate something fully, tidily and definitively.

You will also be more effective in making each intervention tell if you are prepared to work with a few items or issues rather than trying to cram everything in. The more material you cover, the more stories you let yourself tell or listen to, the more you will get lost in the content, and the more 'white noise' you will be creating around your work. It's better to spend your time on one or two key questions, to allow silent time for exploration and reflection, than to get caught up in 'busy work'.

Finally, how you intervene as coach at the end of a session can make a huge difference to what the client will be taking away in terms of learning, insight or action plans. Tim Gallwey found that when at the end of a session he asked his clients to pinpoint what they had learnt they remembered their learning more and were able to use it more effectively.

If you are a coach and ask your clients to 'wrap up' each session in this way, be mindful that the words you use will shape what they do. Asking a client to identify 'what you have learnt' will get you a different result than asking 'what you have found useful'. We like the more open phrase 'what you will take away'. It points the client in the direction that in the end is likely to be most valuable to them. It's also salutary because sometimes what they take away is quite different from what might have been expected! And that can become part of a coach's own learning and reflective self-development. As a client, once you have been asked such a question and discovered how articulating your learning can help engrain it and deepen its value, the habit can become part of your self-coaching apparatus in any learning situation.

At its best, coaching is an economical and focused process. Now we want to focus on some of the most useful interventions.

Essential tools for coaching

What are the essential tools you need to have in your toolkit if your work is to achieve the purposefulness, flexibility and effectiveness that characterise outstanding coaching?

The seven essential tools that we describe have been well tested in practice – so much so that each relates to one or more of the Professional Core Competencies developed by the International Coach Federation (ICF) and used as the foundation for their credentialing process. Whether you are a coach, a commissioner of coaching for others or a client, what follows highlights best practice. Exploring these tools will deepen your understanding of the coaching process that is coaching and offer pointers for enhancing it further.

The ICF Professional Core Competencies are usually listed under four main headings:

A. Setting the foundation
B. Co-creating the relationship
C. Communicating effectively
D. Facilitating learning and results
(The full definition of these competencies and their related behaviours is included as part of the Appendix.)

This list and the chapters in this section itemise a number of absolutely fundamental components of coaching. However, this does not mean that they necessarily occur in a set order. Trying to use them in that way would make coaching strangely mechanical, impersonal and ineffective. So while beginning by designing an alliance is a very good place to start any coaching relationship – and is indeed the first component we examine – after that the other elements can interweave in endless permutations. Coaching utilises a number of processes. It doesn't follow a preordained or sequential pattern, either over the entirety of work with a particular client or even in a single session; but good coaching will contain all of these elements – and not just once. This includes designing the alliance which periodically will be reviewed and frequently redesigned as the coaching continues.

Think of the seven key themes that we have singled out as different-coloured threads that interweave through every coaching session. Sometimes one will stand out for a while, sometimes another.

Sometimes one colour lies above the others, sometimes it dips behind them – but it's always there. Each is distinct, yet each supports the others. For instance, if you haven't designed the working alliance, you won't have the trust that enables you to offer, or to accept, the challenges that may form part of articulating what's going on. If client and coach aren't in the right mind–body state, they won't be able to take the action forward ... and so on. These processes are the essential ingredients that together make up the recipe for good coaching. Their proportions will vary in any coaching session, but they all need to be present to some degree.

In order to help you work with these tools more easily, we present them in a standardised format using the following headings:

1. What do we mean by this tool? What does it look like in practice?

2. What does this tool achieve?

3. Think of using this tool when ...

4. How you can use this tool.

We conclude each account with a list of MultiModal pointers that can potentially broaden the scope of how to make best use of each element.

Chapter Four

Design the Alliance

Empowerment is not something you give me or I give you: we co-construct it between us by the actions each of us takes.

Paul Jackson & Mark McKernow, *The Solutions Focus*, Nicholas Brealey, 2002, page 11

E very person is unique. This means that to make the most of what coaching can offer, you need to customise it. Ideally every coaching partnership will be specially tailored to the needs of the client. Because coaching works through a negotiated partnering, it must begin with negotiation not just about the aims or even the methods, but first of all about the nature of the relationship between the coach and client – or between the commissioner, client and coach. Usually, designing the alliance begins with a quite explicit discussion in the first meeting – sometimes even earlier – in response to an initial enquiry from the commissioner or client. It's truly the foundation of any work they do together. It will include the structural details that form the basis of the contract between the parties (e.g. length and frequency of sessions, fees and place of meeting), but it will also cover issues such as aims, measures of success, roles and responsibilities.

Designing the alliance isn't something that only happens at the beginning. Coach, client and commissioner all need to recognise that any working relationship evolves over time – and that how the parties can best work together may therefore also change over time. So at any point it may be time to redesign …

Your behaviour rests on, reinforces and broadcasts your beliefs. Suppose you turn up late for every coaching session and quite often forget to show up at all. This behaviour will send a message – as will being prepared and on time. What you do enacts your beliefs and will trigger others to make meaning out of your behaviour.

The same applies to the structures we put in place in our lives and in our interactions with others. So at the beginning of their work together some coaches may ask their clients to prepare for a session by thinking in advance what they want to talk about. Like other patterns, this can become a self-maintaining habit, and these clients will often then continue to come along with a personal 'agenda'. Many coaches begin sessions by asking something like 'What would you like to get from today's session?' Why? Because this kind of question creates its own structure by presupposing a number of important things:

- That you *will* get something from it.

- That it's your choice that matters.

- That in articulating what it is you want you will be creating a focus that keeps you on track and helps you get it.

In coaching, agreeing on aims and practical arrangements has much deeper implications than may at first appear. Designing the alliance isn't just a matter of agreeing the framework for coaching as a precursor to getting down to the 'real thing'. It's actually *part of* coaching itself. It *is* coaching in action and not surprisingly is therefore an ongoing process.

Finding a way of agreeing the terms of engagement so that everyone is clear about what they are and that they have co-created them means you're doing something that doesn't happen very often in everyday life either at work or at home. When you step back and start thinking about how you want to do things there are all sorts of things to consider. For instance, is it acceptable for client or commissioner to phone the coach between agreed sessions, and what procedure should be followed if either needs to postpone a session, or if the client wants to ask for an additional or urgent one? What happens if a client has to cancel at short notice? In what circumstances will the client or the company be expected to pay? Is the coach expected to report back to the commissioner – and if so what may they say: how is confidentiality to be respected?

When you think about it there are all sorts of things you might want to clarify. To illustrate we'll focus on just three – payment, the medium used for coaching and location. With payment who pays, and when? If a company is involved, it's going to be important to be clear how often the coach should invoice it, and whether the fee is paid upfront or retrospectively. If the client is paying privately, do they pay in advance or for each session at the time, or perhaps for a number of sessions (e.g. a month ahead)? These are the kinds of questions that need answering at the very beginning.

Then there's the medium used for coaching. Does coaching take place face to face, over the phone – or even by email? Some people are happy to work over the phone, while others much prefer meeting face to face. That said, many people are surprised to find that they really rather like telephone coaching – and not just for its convenience. They say they can really focus. Some say they're able to speak more freely.

As for location, where should the coaching take place? At the coach's office? At the client's workplace? In an agreed neutral venue such as a hotel? Many arrangements can work, but each will create a different experience of coaching, and this needs thinking about before coaching begins. Some clients feel uncomfortable being coached at work, either because they prefer the arrangement to be kept from colleagues or because they can't easily switch their attention from immediate issues and tasks. Coaches, too, may have their own preferences. In itself, coaching can take place just about anywhere, and can be effective whether it is formal or very informal.

Coaching can be wideranging, exploratory and in many ways open, or it can be tightly targeted and highly specific. Either way, there will come a point where its end is in sight. Even in a single half-hour session, a good coach will signal this, often quite explicitly, so that there is enough time to summarise what's been learnt and what the client may need or wish to do in the interval before the next session. This isn't just a question of wrapping up for the sake of being tidy. Wrapping up is much more important than that. Tim Gallwey found in the 1970s that when clients summed up for themselves what they had learnt from a coaching session they retained it more. Putting learning into words helped it to become not only a part of them, but also a part of them that they could continue to use. In naming it they had made it truly their own.

As you can see there are many different possible structures and patterns for arranging coaching. Whichever ones you agree on, most of the time it will probably be the case that outstanding coaching will meet the following minimal criteria.

- It will most likely be regular – to create and maintain good habits, and to encourage a flow rather than a stuttering, stop-start game of catch-up.

- It will give you enough time to identify and explore issues and to find ways of taking them forwards.

- It will make room for ongoing, consistent self-reflection – as well as urgent problem-solving.

- It will not be random, as and when or crisis-led. You will be able to agree a format and number of sessions from the outset. Once agreed, you will engage in the session even if 'there doesn't seem much to talk about' – because coaching is about engaging in the process, not about just having items of content to get through. (Often, it's in the 'not much to talk about' sessions that people get the most value. They take a step back and get a broader perspective on themselves and their situations.)

What do we mean by designing the alliance? What does it look like in practice?

While its co-partners – that is, the commissioner, coach and client – have different roles and their own unique natures, coaching assumes an equality of personal worth and of commitment to each other and to the process. It therefore has to be founded upon mutual agreement. Why are we choosing to work together? What are we seeking? What can we achieve? What evidence will tell us that we are achieving it?

Good coaching begins as it means to go on – as a collaborative endeavour upon an agreed basis. The word *alliance* reflects how it is to experience an excellent coaching relationship. Your coach is on your side. You have an advocate. This alliance is *designed*: it doesn't just occur randomly. Once designed the alliance will almost certainly evolve – it's not uncommon for there to be a change in focus or outcomes as the coaching goes on. Indeed, this ability to change the terms of the alliance by mutual agreement in the light of on-going experience is frequently a very important part of what a client gets from coaching. Many people have told us how novel and liberating they found it and that they were able to apply this way of doing things to other areas of their lives. Instead of feeling boxed in they were able to restructure the modus operandi they had with their colleagues, their spouses and even their children.

To design an alliance is to engage in a collaborative process that explores and sets the rules of engagement for the partnership. This is so whether it's between commissioner and coach, commissioner and client or coach and client. A designed alliance ensures that the rules of engagement are first made explicit and agreed to by both parties. They are then followed and respected and modified by design rather than by accident or through default. The best coaching alliances are tailor-made by and for the individuals involved. They are founded on clarity and agreement between all parties from the outset. For this reason, they may involve a meeting between all interested parties where the rules of engagement are explicitly stated, and even outlined in written form.

Designing the alliance typically begins the first time the commissioner and/or client encounter the coach. This may be through an initial telephone call or perhaps an email, or during a face-to-face meeting. Good coaches and commissioners recognise that even where these discussions are tentative, exploratory and informal, they are starting to lay the foundation for the work that may follow. In other words, designing the alliance has already begun.

What sorts of things are involved?

1. The coaching agenda.

2. Goals.

3. Assessing progress.

The coaching agenda

Coaching at its best works to the client's agenda. Sometimes this is quite explicit from the outset, while at other times it emerges as part of the coaching process. Such an agenda will include such things as specific issues that the client needs to address and goals they may want to achieve. Where organisational commissioners are involved, it can be particularly important to explore 'ownership' of the agenda at an early stage, and to make explicit any divergences between organisation and individual. Resolving such differences becomes an agenda item in its own right. For example, one firm we knew wanted a staff member, Jimmy, to become more involved in developing a new product, and hired in a coach because his manager felt he just wasn't committed to doing this. The coach soon found Jimmy was indeed much more interested in taking another project forward – the one he had been originally headhunted to do!

The agenda frames the coaching and determines what is relevant. If the coaching is work based, is it acceptable to discuss non-work topics and issues? In life coaching, where will the boundaries be drawn between coaching and possible therapy? What is it appropriate to include – and what needs to be ruled out? In both executive and life coaching good coaches generally help their clients to stay forward focused, and will through experience have developed a sensitivity to issues that need unpacking or resolving through therapy instead of coaching. They are likely to draw the client's attention to the 'borderline' status of issues like this, and invite the client to think about seeking a different kind of help. One of the marks of a really good coach is that they know when to refer clients to other professionals!

Goals

What is the coaching aiming to achieve for the individual, and, if one is involved, for the organisation? Are the goals actually achievable? How will any of the partners know when the goals have been achieved? What will tell them if they are going off-track?

Asking questions like these can actually be a powerful coaching intervention in itself, because it breaks down easy assumptions about what's intended, hoped for or fantasised about and gets people to be specific. For example, if someone's goal is to 'be more patient with the children' or 'more accessible to my team', it's going to be important to know what will actually be different when this is achieved. Asking questions like 'How will you know when you've accomplished this?' targets what is actually meant by abstract words like 'patience' and 'accessibility', as they are used by *this* person in *this* context. Such questioning gets us thinking in a different way and from different angles. Doing this can also pinpoint potential areas of misunderstanding ahead of time: you think you are accessible because you read your emails every day, but someone else thinks you are inaccessible because they're never able to catch you on the phone or find you in person.

Assessing progress - focus and review

Focus

Coaching needs to have a clear and tight focus, one element of which is an agreement to be mindful of how far and how fast it is helping the client progress towards their goals. Coaching may seem discursive at times, and indeed some issues and insights need space in which to arise and be explored. But good coaches always remain mindful that time spent needs to be time that repays, so they will be monitoring relevance and value at many levels, and encouraging the client to do the same. 'Why are we talking about this, do you suppose ...?' 'I notice that this topic/pattern has come round again ...'

Review

It seems obvious that where coaching has a specified time frame there will need to be a review towards the end. How are the partners doing? What needs to be done in the remaining time to ensure that agreed goals are met? But long-term coaching also needs to have a review process built in, because it sharpens the focus and ensures that the work is productive rather than discursive. It's rare in our experience that organisations arrange coaching on an 'open' basis without at least a notional time frame: often, indeed, they will set quite specific and tight frames by specifying an exact number of sessions. Even where such boundaries are quite elastic, a good coach will ensure that reviewing progress, even briefly, is a regular part of the work. Good coaching has energy and pace, and this is one way to generate it. Think of the difference between telling yourself you really must get around to something and having a specific deadline for doing it: which is the most likely to help you get the task done?

What does designing the alliance achieve?

Whatever your role, participating in designing the alliance ensures that you have ownership of the process. It increases the investment you are willing to make at many levels, giving you motivation to continue when you are under pressure or when things are hard. Sharing ownership reinforces a sense of equality among the partners that supports their collaboration and encourages openness and willingness to take risks. For the coach, this may make it easier to acknowledge their limitations, to avoid the temptations of 'being the expert', to follow and support the client, and to model attitudes and behaviour rather than tell or exhort. For the client, this makes it easier to try out new behaviours, examine old attitudes and experiment without worrying about having to be successful. For the commissioner, co-defining the scope and aims of the coaching at the outset increases trust and confidence in the coach and client, and in the process itself.

Think of designing the alliance

- When you want to be clear about how you're going to engage with another human being in pretty much any area of your life.

- When you have *any* initial working meeting.

- When you first enquire about coaching.

- When you first meet any of the parties involved in conversations about setting up the coaching.

How you can design the alliance

- Discuss and agree what is appropriate in the relationship and what is not, what is and what is not included, and what your respective responsibilities are for determining and maintaining both content and process.

- Discuss the guidelines and specific parameters of the relationship. In the case of coaching this would involve logistics, fees, scheduling, location, and so on.

- Together determine what is and what is not on the agenda, and how this relates to the time frame available and the goals you plan to work towards.

- Discuss and agree what evidence will tell you that the agreed goals are being achieved.

- If other parties besides the coach and client are involved (for example a commissioner, other team members or the client's family), discuss and agree how you will manage confidentiality and the systemic impact of any changes that may follow.

MultiModal pointers for the commissioner, client and coach

- What Logical Levels seem to be involved in the original brief? Would it be helpful to make explicit use of the Logical Levels model as part of designing the alliance?

- Where the brief is framed in remedial terms, have you discussed its generative possibilities? Is everyone open to a generative approach in the coaching process?

- Have you considered the systemic context of the work and of any changes that may take place as a result of it? What possible resistances or knock-on effects might there be? How are the client's external or internal systems contributing to the core issue, or maintaining it?

- What is the mix between intra-psychic and interpersonal issues here? What information will you both need to be clear about this?

Designing the alliance in practice

What does this look like in the flow of 'real life'? Here are some examples:

▶ **A coach is commissioned to support a newly promoted manager** during her first months in a post as she establishes herself in her role.

The commissioner tells the coach to do whatever is needed to help the manager build confidence and skill. The coach and client agree that the most urgent need is to help her act effectively in relation to a 'difficult' team member and to assist a newer recruit who is finding it hard to get up to speed with his work.

▶ **A life coach is asked to help a man in his thirties** who has just left his partner of seven years having finally recognised that he wants children, although she has always been clear that she doesn't. The coach and client agree that although there are short-term practicalities to be dealt with as effectively and with as little acrimony as possible, the client also wishes to explore longer-term issues about responsibility, guilt, partnering and parenting.

▶ **A doctor seeks coaching through his professional body** to help with stress and potentially addictive habits that have developed during his time in a busy urban practice with a heavy caseload. He and his coach agree to work on issues of life balance and priorities and that he will seek specialist help for treating the developing addiction patterns.

Chapter Five

Get into the Right Mind-Body State

Many key aspects related to implementing a path to a vision ... often occur outside of conscious awareness. They come in the form of insight or inspiration. In addition to instruments and tools that allow us to bring our visions and the path for their realisation into awareness, it is also useful to have some ways of encouraging and actually directing or utilising unconscious processes as well. This is most effectively done through the management of our internal states.

Robert Dilts, *Visionary Leadership Skills*, Meta Publications, 1996, page 31

The state you are in is a composite of your physiology, thoughts and feelings at any one time, and it has profound effects on how you manage yourself in relation to your immediate circumstances and to what you want. If you are agitated you will find it difficult to think clearly. If you are very relaxed you may not react quickly enough. If you are in the grip of strong emotion you may not make the wisest decisions.

There are also other, more subtle dimensions which impact our effectiveness. For example, each of us has familiar or habitual states that we take for granted: enthusiasm, thoughtfulness, anxiety and even depression can become such 'baseline' states that they almost seem to be part of who we are. Yet these states can also change from one moment to another and over time.

So many human activities seem to be conducted in a way that

focuses on subject content at the expense of noticing what's really going on in the people involved. Ignoring or being oblivious to the state the participants happen to be in would fly in the face of everything coaching is about. So in coaching it is vital to pay attention to mind–body states, not least because some of them help the coaching process and some hinder it. Good commissioners 'frame' coaching from the beginning in such a way as to help the client approach it with a mindset that is conducive to reflection, learning and development; good coaches help their clients to be in an appropriate state at the outset of every session; and thoughtful clients may naturally or deliberately arrive in the 'right' frame of mind. However, being in the right mind–body state doesn't have to be a matter of chance or mysterious expertise. It is a skill that you can learn and rely on, whichever role you play. That's the theme of this chapter.

What do we mean by the right mind-body state and what does it look like in practice?

In everyday speech we are used to referring to 'getting in a state' and 'being in the right state' to do something. However, people often don't appreciate that getting into and out of states is something we can personally control.

Good coaches will always explore just how appropriate any given state is to the circumstances a client is dealing with, based on how conducive – or not – it is to managing them. If you are a commissioner, being alert to the mind–body states of potential clients and to the skills of potential coaches in this area will be an important criterion in helping you facilitate good matches between them. If you are a coach or a client it's going to be really useful to get clear about what state you need to be in to give or get the most from coaching – and what you need to do to get into that state.

Examples of the right mind-body state

▶ **Being appropriately proactive when you need to engage others.** One client, a particularly successful manager, scans his audience as he prepares for a presentation: he wants to gauge the kind of state they're in, and find a level of energy that will engage them gradually. In this way he avoids overselling or underenthusing: he gets himself in the right state to get them in the best state.

▶ **Allowing yourself time to reflect at the beginning of a day on what you have to do and what you wish to achieve by the end of it.** You might use natural free-floating states that favour reflection, such as those prompted by familiar activities like having a shower or driving. One client found that when he switched offices his daily driving time was halved. Initially delighted, he was disconcerted to find that after a while he felt more stressed – until he realised that the driving time was when he did much of his most creative musing. The lack of this mental 'space' was making him less effective and so adding to his stress. He needed to create other rituals so that he could put himself in his most reflective and creative state. Only then was he able to once again reap the benefits that come from stepping back and seeing the bigger picture.

▶ **Respecting your body's promptings.** Often a change of physical state will refresh you while allowing your mind to continue unconsciously working on your chosen task. Rather than trying to drive yourself at a constant high-pressure pace all day, you might want to listen to your body's promptings to stretch, get up and have a walkabout, stare into space or take a few quiet moments. Once you have accepted that these impulses can be valuable signals and the space they give you can bring valuable results, it becomes much easier to monitor and respond to them.

▶ **Creating a buffer state between home and work to enable effective re-entry from one world to the other.** One busy professional woman we know closes her eyes for ten minutes or so on the train commuting to and from work each day to give herself space to close down one set of concerns and reorientate herself to the other. She finds that closing her eyes and slowing her breathing (a useful mechanism for deliberately changing states) helps her leave behind her work-oriented state to enter her 'home-oriented one' more easily. This way, she doesn't take work home with her at night. In the morning she uses the same process to help her reconnect with work again.

▶ **Being able to enjoy your successes and achievements rather than**

immediately moving on to the next goal. This has a profound effect upon a person's state. You could achieve this by giving yourself time to enjoy, celebrate and replay the best moments of this or any day. One client learnt to do this in the last moments before settling down to go to sleep. Another made a positive stocktaking something he did each month. If you do either of these you'll change your state quite dramatically. Knowing how to do this can be particularly helpful on a bad day or when you are finding things difficult. By deliberately seeking out the positives, and acknowledging the actual evidence of better things, you can find a situation less overwhelming. Sifting your experience like this can also remind you of deeper values, wider considerations and more lasting truths that help see you through the immediate situation you are struggling with, all of which impacts your state.

By contrast, people who take their successes for granted and simply move on to the next thing don't reap their full benefit and tend to be on an achievement treadmill. Much of the time they'll be in a rather driven state and just upping the ante – more is better. But somehow they never really *feel* satisfied.

▶ **Capture the best for later.** Make the most of good moments: enjoy them in the round at the time rather than letting yourself just pass on to the next thing, and later experiment with recalling them in full detail through all your senses until you find one or two that really do it for you. Then find a key word, phrase or feeling that will act as your rapid personal shortcut to your desired state when you need it. Is this tinkering with 'reality'? Of course – but then so is going over and over something you got wrong, or something someone said or did that hurt you, or endlessly rehearsing what you fear might go wrong. When you do any of these things, you create or engrain states that affect your feelings, attitudes and behaviour just as artificially. Learning to manage your state appropriately helps you put the most into coaching and get the most out of it, whichever role you have – and it also helps you get more out of life.

What does the right mind-body state achieve?

Different activities require us to be in different states, of course. But a good rule of thumb would be that the optimal state for any activity would be that which produces maximum joy and maximum achievement. What is the right state for coaching? By and large, it is a state of alert and speculative attentiveness. How you get to be in this state can vary enormously. Ideally, you'll be calm in body and able to focus your mind in a spirit of reflective awareness and enquiry, not feeling hurried or rushed: you will be quietly alert. You need to have your logical and strategic left-brain processing available – in tandem with your right-brain capacity to feel, imagine and create.

Many times, though, a client may begin a coaching session feeling decidedly frazzled. Coaches have their off days too. Whichever role you're in you need to be able to monitor your own experience as well as simply living it. You need, in other words, to have all of yourself on-line, whether you are coaching or being coached.

The more you can both do this the more you will get from coaching. You can work in depth, if you need to; you can see connections and implications; you can take an overview; you can shift from an awareness of how you are feeling or thinking right now to an awareness of how this connects to other people, the past or the future; you can step outside yourself and consider how you may be perceived by others, examining the effects of different possible courses of actions from their perspective as well as your own.

This is a state of disciplined freedom, of balance that allows you to move when and where you want, of calmness that is yet a readiness to act and to react. Being in this state gives you access to your personal resources and those of your coaching partner. It has a way of slowing time so that even under pressure you can reflect and decide. It keeps you clearheaded and enables you to be openhearted.

Think of the right mind-body state

▶ **When you are about to enter a new, taxing or otherwise important situation.** Ask yourself 'what state do I need to be in to be at my most resourceful?'

▶ **When you are feeling under pressure.** 'Take a deep breath' or 'count to ten before you say anything' are everyday expressions that unconsciously recognise the value of briefly breaking state to give yourself an opportunity to think, inhibit immediate and perhaps unwise responses, and take a different and more strategic tack.

▶ **When colleagues or family are stressed, angry or anxious and you sense that you are beginning to 'catch' their mood even though you don't need to.** You could change your state here by imagining that you are watching the situation from outside, or from a distance: how would that help you feel differently or act more effectively?

▶ **When your state seems inappropriate to the immediate circumstances.** States are always appropriate to *something*, so when you find yourself in some way 'out of synch' with what's going on around you respect the validity of your irritation, your anger, your sadness (or perhaps your elation), and quietly, speculatively, ask yourself what your feeling *does* fit with. Sometimes the answer comes at once, sometimes hours or even days later – but in our experience feelings and reactions that are inappropriate in one situation always have their proper match somewhere.

▶ **When seeking to communicate with someone whose state seems significantly different from your own.** When you notice this kind of mismatch between yourself and another person, you could just wait and see if things improve. Alternatively, you could take the opportunity of getting more on their wavelength by changing your state so that it becomes closer to theirs. Good coaches match the speed of their movements and the urgency of their speech to that of their clients – initially, as a prelude to helping them shift into a more suitable state for their work together. Partners in well-established and effective relationships 'take the temperature' of their partners on meeting up with them after an absence. Children often naturally monitor their parents' mood when they come home from work. Any of these can help preserve harmony, minimise stress, and promote greater collaboration.

▶ **When you want to enhance the pleasure of being alive.** Coaching isn't just about solving problems and managing difficulties. One of its important benefits is that it also helps people make the most of *what already works.* To recognise and celebrate a state that's effective, enjoyable or rewarding is to gain even more from it. To enter a pleasurable situation in a suitable mind–body state is to be even more receptive, even more alert, and even more *alive.*

How to get into the right mind-body state

In our experience, enhancing our skill in managing our own state helps us all, whatever roles we hold at work or in life generally – whether we are a coach, client or commissioner. Here are some suggestions on how you can do this.

- Identify your least favourite states. Find out what triggers them. Consider what elements comprise them and what would be the easiest element to change. For example, you can often change a lethargic or even depressed state by changing your posture, moving around and exercising.

- Get into the habit of monitoring states – both your own and those of other people. Notice what physiology and level of energy tend to go with what feelings, beliefs, thoughts or behaviour.

- Think of a time when your state suddenly changed for the better. Get clear about what caused or helped the change. Practise deliberately triggering this change in low-risk situations.

- Remember a time when you caused or helped someone else to change his or her state. How did you do it? Notice what works for different people.

- Identify some recent occasions when you felt, say, particularly effective, cheerful, relaxed, attentive and able to learn. Consider what helped you get into this state and how you maintained it. Identify any key thought, movement, posture or memory that you might use as a trigger when you want to get into this state again in the future.

- Get clear about what state you want to be in and do what it takes to get into it.

MultiModal pointers

Logical Levels

Environment can certainly have an impact upon the ability of the coach and client to get into the right state for coaching. We are reminded of instances of the daunting impact of large empty boardrooms on nervous clients and novice coaches. Consider what would work best for you. Much of what constitutes desirable *behaviour* in the coach, as far as it facilitates a good coaching state, is discussed in more detail elsewhere in this book.

If you are the client, what can you do? It helps to allow yourself enough time before your session to focus your attention, set aside other concerns and change to a more reflective pace and speculative mood. If you are rushing, mentally or physically, you will be working against the very state you most need. On the other hand, giving your coach a behavioural demonstration of just how hard you're finding it to create space for yourself can sometimes be a very eloquent communication and a good place to start from.

You may already have the *skill* of getting into different states as you need them: if not, it is a skill you can learn, and perhaps one that you might want to develop through your coaching itself.

What *beliefs and values* are involved with accessing effective states? For the coach, a fundamental respect for whatever state the client is in: in coaching there are no right or wrong states, only more and less effective ones.

Coaches provide powerful models to their clients, not just through the words they speak, but also through the unspoken messages of their body language and behaviour. This combination of verbal and non-verbal communication conveys messages directly to the client. Moreover, it offers the client a 'model' of attitudes, values and actions that they can learn to use towards both others and themselves – a model which is all the more subtle because it is natural and pressure free. When good coaches send a consistent message in this complex way that they believe the client's state is understandable, they help the client extend the same acceptance to him or herself. Where emotions such as anger or anxiety are involved, this acceptance can be fundamental in helping a client reach a better understanding with themselves, facilitating change and growth at the level of *identity*.

Remedial-generative continuum

Be aware that a remedial brief may set coaching into a 'catch-up' frame. Sometimes this can produce an adrenal urgency in which the fearful client tries to reform their ways before being fired – be it by their company or by their partner in their personal life. At other times it may send a client into a low-energy, depressed or self-doubting state. Neither condition is really very desirable. Therefore changing the mind–body state may be one of the first important things to do if the resources of both coach and client are to be really accessed.

Systemic perspective

Ask yourself how you will manage your state more effectively, and how perhaps having access to a greater range of states may affect the wider systems of which you're a part. What impact might this have on pre-existing reinforcing or balancing feedback loops? How might they be changed? How can the coach become a model of versatility in state management, so that the client learns how to do the same with his family and colleagues? How could all this give you more leverage in the systems you engage with?

Interpersonal-intra-psychic dimension

Your mind–body state will be affected, sometimes dramatically, not just by the states others are in around you but also by intra-psychic processes within you. In other words, you will be reacting not just to the outside world, but also to your own internal world. Your feelings, behaviour and even physical well-being can all be affected.

Chapter Six

Articulate What's Going On

Often when I am coaching, I let the client know from the outset that my role is not to give advice or counsel and that therefore I don't need any detailed background information of the problem at hand. I simply ask the person to start thinking out loud about the problem and to allow me to 'eavesdrop' on their thought process. I will ask questions or make comments intended to help the person clarify or advance their thinking. This relieves the client of the burden of briefing the coach on the complete picture, and more important, it does not invite a shifting of the responsibility for solving the problem to the coach. The client just starts thinking aloud, and the coach's job is to help the person gain mobility towards his or her desired outcome. Once this understanding is in place between client and coach, the conversation for mobility can usually be completed in a fraction of the time it takes using the traditional model of the coach as problem solver.

Tim Gallwey, *The Inner Game of Work*, Random House, 2002, page 183

C oaching at its best is focused and purposeful, yet like all dialogues it has the potential to become discursive, confused or aimless. Clients can get too close to the content of their issues, and coaches can get sucked in with them too. Or they can collude in avoiding 'difficult' topics, strong feelings, or small slippages in keeping to the coaching contract itself. Coaching can also run into patches of stickiness, stagnation or apparent 'resistance' when dealing with issues of belief and identity. Client and coach can sometimes be overly sensitive or indirect in approaching 'hot' material. Yet failing to approach such areas can mean that coaching, though safe and even reasonably effective, fails to deliver its full potential. This is when good coaching calls for a readiness to 'nail' the issue by articulating it, while at the same time inviting a positive and thoughtful response.

What do we mean by articulating what's going on?

While coaching calls for honesty and directness, putting words to what's happening (or not happening) is not the same as 'speaking your mind'. A skilful coach offers both challenge and security. The challenge is to face reality; the security is that of having support in recognising and working with an obstacle, a block or a limitation. This often involves naming the obvious – although this can seem like a challenge to beginning or unconfident coaches. Articulating what's going on doesn't just stop there: it offers a baseline for further exploration, inquiry, reflection and, ultimately, action. And it is by no means always negative: one of our clients who saw himself as a plain, hardworking, run-of-the-mill guy was astounded to be told how great an asset his absolute and shining integrity was. He was embarrassed at first, because he had taken for granted that this was how one ought to be: recognising how unusual and outstanding he was in this respect – perhaps especially in the cut and thrust of a competitive industry – enabled him to take the next steps towards growing into his full authority as a worker and manager.

What does it take to be this direct? Ultimately, it's a question of being loyal to the truth of the client's world and their experience. Nothing less will do. Fudging in the short term undermines the value of coaching in the long term. The same is true if you are a client. If you feel you have not really been 'heard', if you think that your coach has been leading or pushing you in a direction that isn't yours or that doesn't seem useful, it can be hard to get your courage up to say so; yet if you do so, a good coach will take this as feedback and it will give the two of you an opportunity to get real instead of staying on the surface. It will also help to clear your disappointment or resentment – and probably your coach's sense of frustration or puzzlement – out of the way. The bedrock you both rely on, in articulating what's going on, is a commitment to the partnership and to the process. Strangely, that shared sense of commitment helps both of you tolerate moments where your skill is less than exemplary – where you briefly get it wrong. Because telling it how it is, in this committed way, builds that essential ingredient of coaching and being coached – trust.

In our experience, there are three prime ways of achieving this fresh and effective leverage: Bottom-lining, Intruding and Acting on Intuition. All are initially part of the coach's toolbox; and through the experience of being coached and internalising the skills that are so transparently being used to help her, the client can acquire them for her own future use. If you are the coach, encourage your client to use them; if you are the client, take the risk of experimenting with them, both in your coaching sessions and in your wider world.

Bottom-lining

In accounting, the bottom line is the final figure. You can have spectacular turnover figures but if costs are out of control there won't be much to show for all your labours on the bottom line. So the bottom line is very much to do with what's real. In coaching, it's offering a question or statement that draws attention to the nub of things, whether it's the core of the problem, the summary of a discussion, the report of actions taken or results obtained. It's succinct, clear and contains the essentials. It's a skill that can be used by the commissioner, client or coach.

Intruding

Why would you want to intrude? Surely intruding is impolite? Not if it serves the interests of the client and the process. Coaching is always outcome driven: its aim is to help people manage themselves and their lives more effectively. As a coach, you might want to help a client cut to the chase rather than get lost in lengthy explanations or anecdotes. As a client, you might want to bring your coach back to the 'real' issue if you feel they have deviated or lost you in explanations that don't seem helpful or relevant. Time is of the essence. As coaching partners, you share a desire – and an agreement – to make the best use of the time you have, every time.

Using your intuition

Intuition is a label for the processing that takes place outside conscious awareness, and through associative thinking rather than logical analysis. Often, it seems to be a leap in the dark – going beyond the known. Only later may its relevance or accuracy become apparent. In coaching, we need to be open to both kinds of processing. If you have ever had the experience of wondering 'why am I talking about that?' or of thinking of a story, or an analogy, as someone else was talking, you were catching yourself thinking in this other way.

We have learnt through experience that this unexpected 'arrival' of a thought in consciousness is the result of rapid information processing at an unconscious level, and as such it is always in some way relevant – though not always appropriate for sharing out loud. This is because it sometimes relates to our own feelings or experience rather than to the other person's. So we need to 'sieve' it through consciousness, assessing its relevance before putting it into words, rather than just blurting it out. As coaches, we have both had the experience of offering such an intuitive observation soon after its 'arrival', and of this being found very relevant by the client. Sometimes these are 'in the ballpark' and sometimes they have a literal accuracy.

Wendy remembers a session that focused on a client's dissatisfaction with her current work and other parts of her life, when without any obvious reason she found herself thinking of teashops. On that occasion, she went ahead, saying, ' I don't know why I'm thinking of this, but maybe you'd just be happier running some kind of a teashop.' To which the surprised client replied, 'Do you know, I've always wanted to run a teashop.'

Ian remembers a time when he began to feel mysteriously bored and listless while a client talked about what they said mattered to them. What he actually said was, 'I don't know why, but I'm aware that for the last few minutes I've been feeling bored and drained of energy.' The client paused, and then said, 'Me too.' We can also remember times when we've held the thought before judging the time appropriate to offer it.

Intuition is part of our humanness. As coaches – or clients – we just need to be aware that it isn't invariably right any more than it is wrong. And this is the spirit in which we can offer it – as another way of looking at things, which the client's experience will ultimately prove or disprove. If as a coach you offer an intuitive observation in this way, be prepared for it to either 'land' or sink without trace. If it lands, your client will tell you either in words or in his body language. If it sinks, he will ignore it, brush it off or tell you that it isn't relevant.

What does articulating what's going on achieve?

Articulating what's going on is one of the most powerful and effective tools for getting things clear and getting them moving, and for surfacing what is really at issue. It also builds deep rapport and trust. Clients like supportive coaches who they know will really tell it like it is.

Examples of articulating what's going on

- Pointing out that a client often changes appointment times, and asking her to reflect on why this is.

- Drawing attention to a frequently used metaphor and asking what significance this may have.

- Commenting on discrepancies between what the client is saying in words and in her body language.

- Articulating a frustration when the same issue comes up yet again – and inviting the client to consider what is happening.

Think of articulating what's going on when:

- You feel confused, stuck or off-track.

- You have a sense that more is involved than is appearing on the surface.
- You feel uneasy or dissatisfied with what is happening or not happening.
- You feel that something important is being avoided.

How you can articulate what's going on

Bottom-lining

You can start practising bottom-lining as a silent skill, by listening to someone talking and asking yourself: 'Just what is the gist of this?' When you want to check that you have heard someone accurately, whether it's a set of directions or a description of how they feel, you can offer them a 'bottom-line' summary to check that you have heard correctly. If you get it wrong, the other person will tell you – that's the beauty of it. The key is in the way you frame your statement. If you present your observation as just that, by implication asking the other person to verify that you have understood them and to correct you if you did not, you present minimal threat.

If the other person doesn't respond immediately, but becomes still or perhaps looks absent, take it that you have provoked an internal search. Wait and let them take as much processing time as they need. The principle is the same when coaching on the phone. With practice you will learn to read the quality of the silence on the other end, becoming alert to breathing or small movements that speak volumes.

Key words and phrases for bottom-lining are: Essence, key, gist, issue, core, crux, essential, is that it? Have I got it right? Bottom line.

Intruding

When you feel things have gone on long enough, take an audible breath (this will give your partner warning that you are going to break in), and make your intrusion briefly, clearly and sympathetically. Examples:

'I'm aware that we have only a little time left today and I want to make sure we get the most from it, so let me ask you ...'

'Just give me the highlights – those will be enough for us to work on.'

'Can I ask you to stop for a moment? I notice that ...'

Using intuition

Use words and phrases that make it easy for the other person to accept, or reject, what you are offering. For example:

'I don't know whether this is helpful, but I wonder if ...'

'This may just be my own imagination, but I keep thinking of ...'

'I have this image of ... I don't know whether it may be relevant for you or not.'

'Can I risk making a leap of faith here and say that ...'

'I really haven't any hard evidence for this, but it occurs to me that maybe ...'

If the intuition doesn't seem to land, or if the other person feels it isn't helpful, let it go. It may be that you were wedded to your idea; it may be that they need longer to find the relevance of your observation; it may be that you have picked something up before it has even properly surfaced, and only later will they come back to you with, 'You know what you were saying a while back about such and such, well ...'

MultiModal pointers

Logical Levels

Articulating what's going on is a powerful grounding skill which focuses the coaching process: it may confirm the level on which the partners are already working, or open up other levels – as, for example, when naming a behaviour invites clients to consider what that behaviour may be 'saying' about their beliefs, or their sense of identity or even their mission in life.

Coaching a riding client one day, Wendy commented on an aspect of his posture that was limiting his effectiveness. When he continued riding for some time without attempting to make any adjustment, she pointed out that he wasn't changing – and ventured that he seemed reluctant to do so. The client – who was a professional riding instructor – then explained that he had arrived at his current position after studying a system of training that he believed in and found very helpful. Changing this one thing, to him, implied compromising the rest. They had hit on an issue of belief. Unpacking what this involved for him, and finding a way to change his behaviour without compromising his beliefs, took the session – and his riding – forward, and was only possible because of an intervention that had combined bottom-lining and intuition.

Remedial-generative continuum

Articulating what's going on is an intervention that has a special place on this continuum. In fact, it can be the very fulcrum that makes the shift from remedial to generative. In itself, the 'naming' draws attention to a current behaviour that needs addressing, and to this extent it is remedial. But where the issue is insightfully chosen and tactfully addressed, the way is also opened for new behaviour, new thinking and ultimately for personal transformation.

Systemic implications

Articulating what's going on is a process that involves description and invitation: it moves from what is to what may be or what might be. In this way it offers the opportunity to see a bigger picture and a larger context. (This is what comes with seeing the systemic implications of present behaviour.) It therefore opens up a consideration of how things that are immediate relate to the wider systems of which they are part: the words to the thoughts; the actions to the beliefs; the physiology to the concerns; the here and now to its longer-term implications and consequences.

Interpersonal and intra-psychic

The best coaching cannot help but be a systemic process, whether or not that is its overt focus. The agreed focus of your coaching may be on interpersonal issues, or on the intra-psychic world of the client. But inevitably, wherever you start there will be implications in the other dimension of any person's life. Sometimes, this connection is precisely what is made manifest through a coach, or a client, bottom-lining, intruding or using their intuition to highlight what's really going on.

Chapter Seven

Ask Powerful Questions

> If the coach and the coachee are travelling companions, then the coach's
> questions and listening are the quality of light by which they travel.

Julie Starr, *The Coaching Manual*, Prentice-Hall Business, 2003, page 147

Every question has the potential to focus the spotlight of attention on one aspect of our experience over and above others in that moment. Many of the questions we ask and answer in everyday life are simply looking for factual information, and many questions leave us just the way they found us. But there are other questions that probe a bit further into motivation, preferences and aspirations. In coaching, questions are used as a specific form of intervention: they aim to get the listener thinking, to shift perspective, to discover information he didn't know he had, to speculate, to wonder – to take a new step in growing and transforming himself.

Such questions trigger an internal search in the listener and are a powerful tool in coaching. The coach genuinely doesn't know the answer – and often the client is also surprised. Such questions push the boundaries of their discussion so that together they find themselves exploring genuinely unknown territory. This is where many of the real breakthroughs of coaching occur. A simple question like 'What do you really want?' can have a powerful effect. A client says 'I can't . . .' and the coach asks 'What stops you?'

Another client says 'I've never done that' and the coach asks 'What would happen if you did?'

Powerful questions are initially framed by the coach, but the habit of seeking to go beyond the known, to wonder, to speculate and to delve beneath the surface, is one that clients can rapidly take on board and begin to use for themselves. Often the first sign that this is happening comes when, as happened to Ian, a client reports back 'I wondered "what would Ian be asking me in this situation?" He'd say something like "What really matters to you at this moment?"' This client was consciously using his coach as a model for self-coaching. Over time the process becomes more automatic, as clients give themselves a fractional pause or time out that allows them access to deeper levels of understanding and self-knowledge even when they're in the midst of something. A few seconds are all that's needed to set off the search – and maybe even to find the answer they didn't know they had.

What do we mean by asking powerful questions?

A question has power when it stimulates the listener to new thought; when it asks him to search and go beyond what he already knows; when it requires him to think outside the box; when it helps him to make new connections, and to see familiar things in a new light or from a different perspective. Such questions have great potential leverage and are one of the most valuable tools of coaching. They are not all alike in how they achieve their effects, and so in this section we want to look at three key types of questioning you can employ – inquiring, requesting and asking permission. Then we want to touch on the magic ingredient that can supercharge all three – the investigative power of silence.

Inquiring

Inquiry questions are often questions about values, or about what kind of evidence supports a person's beliefs. They may also get the client thinking about something that's so familiar to them that they've ceased to be aware of it. Values like 'loyalty' or 'kindness', judgements that involve 'oughts', 'shoulds' and 'musts', have often become almost invisible. Coaching can help the client unpack just what it is that they mean by them – and become aware of how other people may use exactly the same word while having a quite different sense of what exactly it equates to in practice. Often these will lead to the big questions. What keeps me going? How do I know that this is so? What would I defend at any price? How do I know what is enough? How would you know that things were beginning to change in the way you want?

Sometimes a coach will end a session with an inquiry. This is an open-ended question. It invites the client to consider a particularly fruitful avenue of exploration – how would life be different if you weren't giving your power away? After a while the client may pose such questions for himself – 'I guess I shall just have to ask myself what keeps me ticking when things are this hard.' Sometimes a coach will be wise enough to ask a client, 'What would be the most useful question I could ask you?'

Inquiries like these often bring up even more questions. They can start off a whole process of exploration and evaluation that simmers from one session to the next and often beyond it. The question both sharpens the focus and forwards the action of the session. One question that Ian's coach gave him to consider which he found really useful was, 'What am I building?' Most frequently, this exploring involves unconscious as well as conscious processing: it may give rise much later to one of those sudden 'Eureka!' moments, where an insight or an image suddenly erupts as if from nowhere into a quite different pattern of thinking. I suddenly realised ... It came to me that ... All of a sudden I saw ...

Requesting

Coaching is a transparent process: it seeks to make its workings evident to the client, and it makes use of a form of question known as 'requesting'. Often in everyday life, the significance of requesting is downplayed – frequently because it's a token announcement of intent rather than genuinely offering the opportunity of saying 'no'. 'Would you mind getting this done by five o'clock?' often really means 'do this by five o'clock'. 'Could you take the kids to school tomorrow?' can actually mean something like 'Now it's your turn.' Genuine requests are different, and they have two stages. The first is the 'alert'. Good coaches often alert clients to what they are about to do. They may say, 'I have a thought that I'd like to share with you ... would that be OK?' or 'I've been wondering whether this might be useful ...' Announcing what you're going to do before you do it alerts someone to what's coming. Such flagging can increase active participation. Only then is it time to move on to the second stage – the actual request. 'I have a request. Would you be willing to ...?'

The initial alert means that the request, when it comes, is more than just a formality. Flagging a request in advance like this conveys to the client that she has a *choice*, and that she has the right to exercise it. This is not always the case in everyday life. How many times has someone else given their opinion without checking if you wanted it, or asked you to do something in the ambiguous format that begins, 'Can you ...?' or, worse, 'Can you just ...?' Buried in that little word 'can', which on the surface means simply 'are you able to?' is the implication 'Will you?' And buried in the word 'just' is the implication that what is being asked is only a small, unimportant thing, easy to comply with, no trouble at all ... It's a masked and actually quite manipulative request, and as such it's hard to resist.

Coaching works to increase people's choices and help empower them in making them. It's therefore important that coaches act in accordance with this key principle. As in so many other ways, making requests open and encouraging real choice can cascade into other areas of the client's life: he becomes more alert to the difference between open and hidden requests that he and others make of each other, more able to defend his choices and reject any that he is uneasy or unwilling about. He is less likely to slip into saying 'yes' and regretting it later, and more aware of the need to respect others by offering them clear and explicit choices, too.

To make effective requests:

- State explicitly that you are about to make a request.

- Make your language simple and direct.

- Put your request first, in straightforward language. Say, for example, 'I'd like you to ...' or 'May I ...' or 'Would you ...'

- Make any explanations or reasons clear and unambiguous.

Asking permission

A good coach respects the agenda he and the client have agreed, and also respects the client's sensitivities. If the coach thinks it will help the client to go beyond the agreed agenda, or if he senses that the client may be uneasy or embarrassed, he asks permission first: 'I sense that you find this topic uncomfortable, but I think it could help to stay with it a little longer. Would you be willing to do that?'

Asking permission means that you accept the person's decision and work with it. If you don't – especially if you attempt to get around to the topic indirectly – you will lose their trust. If they have flagged an area as no-go, then keep out of it. If, on the other hand, they give you permission, seeking it first has enhanced their trust in you and strengthened your partnership and your ability to work together. Sometimes asking permission can help you redesign the alliance: 'Although it wasn't part of our original agenda, I'm thinking it might be useful now to look at what led you to leave your old job. Would that be all right with you?' This is as effective in everyday life as it is in coaching.

Utilising the power of silence

Silence well used can enhance the power of almost any question. Too often people will ask a question and then follow up with distracting supplementals if the listener doesn't respond absolutely immediately: 'What I mean is . . . well, let me put it this way, then . . .' If you've asked a significant question it's not uncommon for the person to actually think about it, go on an internal search and then reply. All this can take time.

Often it is wise to be still and wait, and pay attention. People need time to think, to feel and to reflect. They don't need to be dragged out of their private explorations by a comment, or another question. They don't need to feel hurried, or harried. Sometimes silence is essential for processing. If you are lucky enough to experience or to observe excellent coaching, you may be surprised by how little the coach or client actually says. The extreme version of this is when coaching becomes almost like a shared meditation: the client sometimes speaks and is sometimes silent, and the coach's interventions are like small, though telling, punctuations that simply serve to open up, enhance or confirm the client's uniquely personal journey.

Silence is not a void. It invites. It requires. It provokes. In coaching, leaving a silent space can be an act of encouragement, of sympathetic challenge. It is also a way of paying attention. When the client experiences silences like these, she too begins to value them, and may feel able to request them: 'Just give me a minute more to mull that over ... No, that's not quite it – let me think about this ...'

One of the best ways to become more at ease with silence in dialogue is to train yourself to 'work with' the natural pauses that occur in conversation. Respecting these spaces means waiting to see what they may bring forth, either in yourself or in the other person.

Start collecting powerful questions

Some questions have a disproportionate power to really make you *think*. They send you on an internal search in such a way that you reconfigure your internal experience. Maybe you see things in a way you'd never thought of before. New ways of thinking can produce new ways of being.

Every question is a possible gift. Of course, some gifts are more welcome than others but it's worth starting to collect those that really deliver – and you never know where they're going to come from. Ian's wife, Paulette, had an interesting consultation with a homeopath. Wanting to get a sense of her as a person he asked 'What about your character?' This certainly got her attention but she wasn't too sure what he meant, so he clarified by saying, 'Well, if you were to live with yourself for three months, at the end of that time what would you like about yourself and what wouldn't you like about yourself?' For her this was a dynamite question. It really set her thinking – and as a coach she's asked it of a number of clients since. She was particularly taken with it because, as she said, 'it's one of those questions that you can ask yourself more than once and learn something new each time'.

You'll certainly find useful questions in some of the coaching literature itself, but once you start filtering specifically for questions you'll also be amazed at the gifts that come your way in the course of just living your life. So, heard any good questions lately?

What does asking powerful questions achieve?

Powerful questions invite internal exploration, suggest new lines of enquiry and imply the possibility of fresh commitment. In good coaching, they are offered in a spirit and tone of respectful curiosity. These are not questions to which the coach already knows the answer: that is their magic. This enquiry is genuine. The coach really wants to know – and wants the client to know.

Such questions are very different from those that simply seek additional information or prompt the listener to provide well-rehearsed explanations or invite a yes/no response.

Think of asking powerful questions

- When you feel it is worth probing deeper.

- When you feel a breakthrough is close.

- When you feel you or the other person is stuck in seeing the situation from only one angle and might benefit from having to consider another viewpoint.

- When you want to challenge the other person or yourself.

- When there may be more going on than is apparent on the surface.

How you can ask powerful questions

Timing can make all the difference to the power of a question. Where the client becomes thoughtful and for a moment silent, a prompting question can edge her to explore just that bit further. The pause is a signal that the person is engaged internally.

The question may not even need to be completed. For example, a coach might say: 'Is there anything in common, do you think ...?' or 'What might help you ...?' or 'And then ...?' or 'And if you did ...?' Remember that you can ask a question in your tone, not only in the form of words you use. Recapping and clarifying the gist of what someone has said, with a questioning tone – 'So, you're concerned that x may happen?' – can be very effective. It requires the client to 'go inside' and check whether you have summarised correctly.

What you presuppose in a question may be as important as the question itself. For example, 'So when you've got around this/learnt that/become more skilled at ... What will be the biggest difference?' presupposes both that the person *will* deal with their current issues and that they will do so effectively. The overt question – what will be the biggest difference – may be useful in itself, but it rides on the back of two very influential companions! Be prepared to take a risk and see if together you can go just that bit further, gain that bit more information, take an extra step, go outside the box and consider the situation from another perspective. When requesting be clear and explicit about what you are asking. Where possible, frame your request in positive language – clarifying what you actually want the other person to do. Negatively framed requests do not guide the person as to what behaviour is actually desired. Put positively, a request can act as a 'recipe for success'. Remember that a request can be met with three responses: yes, no and re-negotiate.

MultiModal pointers

Logical Levels

A question that invites the client to shift Logical Levels can often be profoundly effective. For example, if someone is angry or worried about the way another person is behaving and you ask them what kind of principles they feel these actions are violating, you may help them recognise that the dispute is actually one about values, not just behaviour.

Remedial-generative continuum

As we've seen, questions are a main means of creating leverage. A powerful question offered in a remedial context can sometimes shift the work towards the generative end of the continuum. For example, 'So what might be the difference between continuing this pattern in the future and finding a new way to handle this kind of situation? And who would you be then?'

Systemic implications

When people are focused on the here and now of their immediate situation, powerful questions that specifically lead them into thinking systemically can be an effective means of helping them enlarge the context of their thinking. For example, 'So how will this impact the larger system?'

In families, partnerships and organisations, it is really helpful to be asked to consider just how your individual experience may be shaped by, or be shaping, the macro system of which you are part; to reflect on what maintains the status quo; to search for the smallest point of leverage that will be effective; to consider how your concerns may be impacting that most vital of all micro systems – your body; to explore how improving the quality of the way you live could make you more effective. All of these can be approached through questions. Looking at systemic implications might simply involve asking, 'How might your children be feeling about this?' In another context it might mean asking, 'And if you imagine how this decision might look in a year's time ...?'

Above all, powerful questions that invite you to explore the meaning of events and reactions as feedback rather than as badges of 'success' and 'failure' can help create a lastingly different attitude towards your experience.

Interpersonal-intra-psychic

One role of powerful questions is to invite someone to explore an area that is unfamiliar or neglected. While most clients and commissioners would assume that coaching could help with interpersonal issues, many people are not accustomed to 'reading' their own physiology, and miss signals that could give them warning or confirmation about what is going on. Powerful questions can help bring a change of focus. For example, 'Just what, do you suppose, is your back-ache telling you right now?' People can also be helped to 'read' their own behaviour differently. For example, 'And what might that "lazy" part of you be trying to achieve for you, do you think?'

Chapter Eight

Forward the Action

> 'Sometimes these small steps may feel almost insignificant but they build up to create something new. This is what life is like, it is lived in tiny steps. At what point does a young person become old? When does a stream become a river? Where exactly is the foot of a mountain? Where does the mountain start?'
>
> Anthony M Grant & Jane Greene, *Coach Yourself: make real change in your life*, Momentum, 2001, page 140

Coaching is often thought of as a process that helps someone get from A to B, and in that sense most people would see it as an activity that's largely about developing purpose and generating action. But while coaching is about movement and purpose, outstanding coaches know that it's not about ticking the boxes on one more to-do list. This can just lead all the partners into making short-term, superficial or cosmetic changes rather than profound, lasting and truly transformative ones – there may be a lot of activity but that doesn't mean it's really forwarding the action. To really take things forward you'll be going deeper than this, as we shall see.

What does it look like in practice?

When you examine what happens in outstanding coaching, it becomes clear that forwarding the action is absolutely fundamental. In a sense all coaching processes – including reflecting, exploring, pausing, being silent, wondering and allowing yourself to 'not know' – are all ultimately in the service of the client being able to live more effectively in the world. All good coaches find ways to encourage commitment and involvement, whatever may be going on at a particular moment. This active, living quality of purposeful engagement comes about through the quality of attention given, through focusing and through keeping to the agenda. It means relating what you are doing to the outcomes you are seeking. And so, of course, it can also involve bringing yourself back when you sense you are off-track.

So a coach or client might set the tone at the very beginning of a session by asking a question such as:

'What would you like to get from our session today?' or 'I'd like to use today's session to help me with ...' rather than 'What's been happening since we last met?' or 'Let me update you ...'

Starting off like this ensures that from the very beginning there's a focus and an objective – both defined by the client. There's therefore an extra pay-off, too: because she has set the framework for the session, she feels much more ownership of it and of what happens within it. Similarly, when a coach (or commissioner) reminds a client that only a few sessions of the contract remain, and asks them to decide how these could best be used in relation to the agreed goal, this helps all parties to ensure that the remaining time is used most effectively, and the course of sessions continues to feel purposeful to the end rather than just petering out or breaking off.

Forwarding the action gives the client the responsibility of taking himself seriously, of making the time, of doing the work and of addressing the issue, but also of being willing to experiment and to take the results as feedback.

It is a coach's job to help the client stick to the client's own agenda – or to recognise that it needs changing. 'You know, when we began working together you fully intended to pass that German exam; but you've talked less and less about it, and I sense that your enthusiasm has waned. If it has, then maybe this isn't the time, or it's not for you?'

Putting words to an issue like this can help a client let himself off the hook – or alternatively reconfirm his intention and begin to find out just what is getting in the way of him following through.

Forwarding the action means helping the client go that extra mile – for example, by asking questions like, 'What's the next step?'... And what will you do then?' These questions can 'raise the bar' and help the client discover that she can manage – and achieve – more than she thought she could. (There's more about this in Chapter 9.)

In this section we will highlight some specific ways in which you can forward the action. As with so much in coaching, these tools will initially be modelled by the coach or commissioner's approach to the client, but increasingly become habitual and therefore part of the client's own repertoire of skills for self-coaching. Some key skills involve:

- Goal setting and planning.

- Finding patterns and structures that support the client in working to her agenda and helping her put these in place.

- Challenging the client to stretch further or aim higher.

- Holding the client accountable.

Goal setting and planning

In most people's minds this is perhaps the most obvious way of forwarding just about any action. An organisation may want an employee to improve the way he manages his team; a worker may want to get promoted; an about-to-be divorcee may want to manage the separation well for the sake of the children; a 45-year-old may want to get into another career.

Coaching needs to help the client (individual or corporate) evaluate whether the goal is achievable, whether they are prepared to put in what it takes to get there, what sequence of smaller steps will build up into that bigger achievement and what else will be needed to help. Coaching may also check whether the steps are within the client's own power to achieve. For example, it may be one of the coach's first steps to get an employer to recognise that achieving the firm's goal will only be possible if it is also meaningful for the client. 'We want her to put more into the part of her job she seems less committed to' will only be a valid goal if the client can be helped to find a way to *be* more committed.

One specific strategy that can help clients achieve their goals is to work with them to create a step-by-step action plan that works backwards from their ultimate goal. Suppose the goal is to change career. Today's first step might be to contact three colleges to gather information about entry as a mature student.

Sometimes a client's goal may be unrealistic – perhaps he has no means of ensuring that he can get the promotion that he wants, or even deserves: there may be other comparable candidates, or there may be a hiring freeze ... What then? Coaching will need to address the feasibility of the desired goals before moving on. In some cases, forwarding the action may mean recognising which actions can't be forwarded – and then finding out what can!

What we do know is that articulating goals clearly, working out what can be done today, tomorrow, next week and next month to progress towards them, and being prepared to adapt, monitor and re-evaluate the current situation in relation to those longer-term ends, gives you a better chance of achieving what you want. Putting your goal into words and sharing it with another person clarifies it and helps it act as a compass point by which to steer.

Finding patterns and structures

The ancient Greek philosopher Aristotle suggested that we are what we repeatedly do, and that consequently excellence can become a habit. One very helpful thing coaching can achieve is to identify habitual actions and patterns that can or could further the client's personal journey towards greater excellence – and those that couldn't. Some of these may be very simple: backing up your computer work at the end of every day, for example. What habit will help you do that? That habit is potentially a very useful structure.

Some structures are more subtle and more far-reaching in their effects than others. One of our clients found that this one really worked for her. She would take 15 minutes at the beginning of each week to envisage what she wanted to achieve by the end of it. Then she would begin each of the remaining weekday mornings by focusing for five minutes on what she wanted to get done that day – by lunchtime, by the end of the day – and how this would contribute towards achieving the goal she had set for the week. Where circumstances forced her to amend the plan, these regular brief reflections allowed her to adjust for reality and yet keep focus and momentum.

Scheduling is so often a structure that can support you in taking steps towards your goals, enabling you to become more professional and more effective. Ian has found many times that one of the most powerful things that can prevent clients losing weight is that they have not planned ahead for when they will be hungry. Suddenly they need to eat and grab whatever is to hand. Learning to be prepared and have sugar-free snacks and appropriate meals ready ahead of time requires forethought every single day, not just once in a while. That usually requires putting a new structure in place.

Another example would be finding ways to get important jobs done. Many people tend to do small jobs first, so they accomplish lots of small jobs but often at the expense of the more important ones. Finding structures that help with the big tasks is a matter of experimenting, and of working with the way you naturally think and behave. For instance, an alternative structure which we've found works well is to take small chunks of available time to 'eat holes' in big tasks. That way, you make sure that you do slowly but surely get the important things done. You are structuring your use of available time to support the more vital tasks.

Piggybacking an existing structure can be a good way to add a new item to it: for example, most people have regular times for showering or cleaning their teeth, and find it relatively easy to make this natural downtime a space for planning or reflection. Regularity is the key to habit formation. How can you install a habit that will enhance your effectiveness?

Knowing the way you naturally think can be helpful. For instance, if you are particularly visual, use visual prompts and visualise how you want to behave. We have known students who wore particular clothes for lectures, presenters who found a personal 'uniform' that enhanced their confidence when they were presenting (both kinaesthetic prompts), and a doctor who signalled his readiness to listen by pushing his swivel chair back from his desk and turning to face his patients. And it's been shown that young people can study more effectively when listening to classical music (an auditory prompt). All these proved to be helpful structures.

Challenging the client

Forwarding the action gives the coach the responsibility of deciding when she needs to confront or challenge the client, or to bottom-line (see Chapter 6). Challenging the client grows out of a belief that they have it in them to achieve even more, that they are even more able and more resourceful than they know or currently demonstrate. Successful challenging doesn't mean changing the goalposts: that can rob people of their right to enjoy successes. Rather, it goes hand in hand with a true appreciation that the coach reflects both verbally and non-verbally and encourages the client to show towards himself. Challenging is about testing if the sky truly is the limit. This is very different from the dreary, unspecified 'could do better' of the school report.

A good guideline for challenging sympathetically and appropriately is to remember that people have two fundamental needs where learning and performance are concerned: they need to feel safe, and they need to grow. Between these two is a constant push-pull dynamic, which you can learn to recognise and work with. You might think of it as a continuum that extends from a comfort zone ... through a stretch zone ... on out into a panic zone.

When someone is in their comfort zone they're probably under performing: certainly, they're unlikely to be developing. But they will not be stressed. They could even begin to get bored. The key growing areas for plants are in the tips of their roots and shoots: those are their stretch zones, and people, similarly, are in their stretch zone when they are working towards the edge of their capabilities. Sometimes this happens naturally in everyday life, when circumstances make demands – and people are amazed that they have the ability to meet them. On the other hand, the demand is too great if you're stretched too far, or for too long. Then you may end up in your panic zone, where learning ceases and performance deteriorates.

The art of coaching, whether you are working with yourself or with someone else, is to use the comfort zone regularly but fairly briefly for reliable performance, ease and refreshment, to move into the stretch zone with regular invitations to discover just how much more might be achieved, or learnt or discovered, and to respect and respond to the first signals of concern that indicate approaching overwhelm.

If you are a coach, part of your work involves edging your client towards more and better. Finding she can do that bit extra can be really empowering, just as doing those last few repetitions in a workout can show you what you're made of. If she looks alarmed or sounds doubtful at this point, invite her to say what she thinks *would* be possible. That way, she commits to a stretch rather than sliding into a panic. The same respect should be applied in self-coaching. In challenging and negotiating challenges, be specific. How much? How many? How often? By when? That way, the challenge can be met. After all, who knows what 'could do better' really means?

A coach might become aware, for example, that a client is tending to avoid conflict, or finds it hard to speak up for herself or her beliefs, and says something like, 'I sense that you may be dodging this conversation because you expect it to be difficult. If that's the case, what would help you do what you have been avoiding up till now?' People can find it hard to speak 'good' truths, too, and a coach might usefully challenge the client to express their appreciation of a friend/colleague/partner in words rather than remaining silent.

Holding the client accountable

Accountability is one of the fundamentals of coaching. While it's true that the coach is accountable to the client for using their skills as best they can, the primary focus of accountability is with – and for – the client.

Often a coach will design the alliance with the client so that he can hold the client accountable. However, there's accountability – and then there's Accountability. In our working lives we are used to being held accountable. But, while on a day-to-day basis we're held accountable, who is holding us Accountable for making sure we tend to what matters most in our lives? Too often the minutiae are scrupulously monitored but the degree to which our life is honouring – or not honouring – our personal and most cherished values is overlooked.

When training coaches, Ian often suggests they think of themselves as the custodians of their clients' primary values. These will be elicited in the initial session. In our view one of the primary contributions the coach can make is to be mindful of the client's values and ensure that they don't get swamped by the demands of the day. The coaching space is one place where we can reconnect with what matters most to us – and then ensure that it has a place in shaping our choices in the days ahead.

Who is a client accountable to? Ultimately, to himself, because if he lets himself down, he is also letting down his employers, partners or family. However provided and paid for, coaching is a process aimed at developing more effective self-management. Genuine commitment to this aim and engagement in the process that facilitates it is the ultimate test of client accountability – irrespective of external achievements or progress.

What does forwarding the action achieve?

The ICF document on Coaching Core Competencies provides us with some succinct examples:

> *9b. Helps the client to focus on and systematically explore specific concerns and opportunities that are central to agreed-upon coaching goals.*
>
> *c. Engages the client to explore alternative ideas and solutions, to evaluate options, and to make related decisions.*
>
> *d. Promotes active experimentation and self-discovery, where the client applies what has been discussed and learned during sessions immediately afterwards in his/her work or life setting.*
>
> *f. Challenges client's assumptions and perspectives to provoke new ideas and find new possibilities for action.*
>
> *h. Helps the client to 'do it now' during the coaching session, providing immediate support.*

Each of these is worded as a description of things that occur in the coaching process – yet it simultaneously tells us some of the important things that coaching can achieve. It is almost as though these occur as a by-product of the overt agenda – for example, managing my team more effectively, learning how to be a better husband, discovering my creative side. As a result of his coaching sessions, the client gets to be a better team manager *and* to explore alternative solutions to old problems; to learn how to be a better husband *and* to find new possibilities for action – not just in regard to the initial 'problem' but in every sphere of his life.

Think of forwarding the action

- Whenever you want to focus attention.

- Whenever there is agreement about goals. What will be the next step? When will it be taken?

- Whenever you feel confused or stuck. What will help you move forward?

- When you seem to have reached a plateau: is this time for a change of strategy? For a new action plan? For a brainstorming session? For experimenting?

How you can forward the action

- Draw attention to the need for action, for follow-up or follow-through.

- Put words to your doubts, or your hesitation or your disappointment. Ask if your partner feels the same. Open up a discussion about options.

- Cultivate the habit of seeking multiple solutions rather than settling for the first one that comes along.

- Be specific and encourage your partners to be the same.

MultiModal pointers

Logical Levels

Forwarding the action means being alert to implications and connections between different levels. Where you encounter an obstacle, ask yourself what level it's on. Sometimes it's a belief that is holding an unwanted or limiting behaviour in place: you'll move much faster if you switch your attention to the belief rather than plugging away at trying to change the behaviour. If someone is underperforming, maybe this is not due to lack of skill but to fears of what success might mean for them.

Remedial-generative

When you have a remedial brief, one way to forward the action is to keep alert for any possibility of working more generatively. Coaching is about movement: once things are improving – where next? It can be really helpful to discuss this explicitly in coaching. The principle of looking to the next steps can help you move from a catch-up situation and the feelings of inadequacy that go along with it to the excitement of discovering just how far it is possible to go.

One client we worked with on the remedial brief of 'improving communication' found that as he learnt to anticipate how other people would receive what he said, and to fine-tune the way he put things to make it easier and more acceptable for them, he began to build networks and find a new confidence in becoming 'visible'. Small increments in interpersonal skill built him a better profile within his organisation, so that the following year he was put forward for promotion.

Systemic implications

Forwarding the action involves the continual monitoring of the relationship between the present and the future, and between the individual and the different systems they're part of. A young client of ours was working in London although her home was in Australia. She had deliberately chosen to make this move because it gave her the opportunity of furthering her career through working in a world-class organisation. However, she missed her extended family greatly and planned to return some day – if only she could find the right opening at the right time and for the right salary. She wanted our help in either firming up a decision to stay (and, by implication, feel less conflicted) or to put her energies into finding a new post back home.

Through our sessions together the client was able to realise that she didn't have to make an either/or choice: she could work hard at developing in her current post through hard work, while *at the same time* working towards her goal of returning home by using some of her weekends and evenings to study for an extra qualification that would broaden her portfolio of skills, and by networking regularly with people in the same field in Australia. She found with great relief that she didn't have to give up either goal: she could work towards both at once.

Looking for opportunities to take things forward means that you have the chance to increase the possibilities of impact on the system, whether individual or interpersonal. 'The longest journey begins with a single step' – and when you are mindful of your direction and move towards it whenever you can, you are likely to be maximising your systemic leverage. This is a tool that needs careful monitoring: will purposefulness be misunderstood as relentless ambition? Will taking every opportunity come across as hustling? Will that new exercise regime, applied so eagerly, actually become exhausting and debilitating or make the family feel neglected?

Systems theory reminds us that the speed of change is dictated by the *slowest* element in any system. Our hopes usually tell us that it should happen at the speed of the fastest. Forwarding the action may sometimes involve reminding yourself that change is often best thought of as a rolling programme rather than a series of discrete steps: that way, you can put energy into the continuous nurturing of anything that contributes to your goal-seeking.

Interpersonal-intra-psychic

Often there is a parallel between what is going on between you and others and what is going on within yourself. For example, people who drive others relentlessly are likely to be intolerant of their own shortcomings or backslidings. A young man we knew who was impatient with his colleagues took his own skills so much for granted that he was never satisfied with his own performance, expected a lot of his wife and bought an expensive piano for his children – even though they were too young to play – because 'they should learn to play an instrument'. His coaching was focused on developing his skills as a manager, but because his coach helped him understand this interpersonal–intra-psychic connection, and encouraged him to monitor it, he came to recognise that he could take some of the pressure off and actually become a better manager – not just of his staff but of himself. As he started to do this he became less demanding and more encouraging. Not only did his team's morale and performance improve, but also he began to appreciate his family.

Chapter Nine

Champion the Client

Imagine a relationship in your life with a person who is sometimes even more committed to what you want in your life than you are. Imagine what it would be like if someone knew your values and life purpose and was holding you true to them – someone who would hold the flag at the top of the hill, encouraging you to press on, someone to celebrate your victories and help you learn from your setbacks.

Laura Whitworth, Henry Kimsey-House & Phil Sandahl, *Co-Active Coaching,*
Davies-Black Publishing, 1998, page xix

The evening before we began writing this chapter, a supervision colleague phoned: 'You remember that feisty young woman I talked about in supervision some months ago? Well, she really took on board what her colleagues had been saying about her manner and worked on her interpersonal skills. Yesterday she phoned me and said she'd gone for promotion – and what's more, she got it! She's Assistant Director now.'

This young woman had not been an easy client. But her coach had worked with her as she was, building trust through a judicious mix of accepting her at the Logical Levels of identity and beliefs while often challenging her at the levels of capability and behaviour. She had, in essence, been conveying a consistent message: you are fine as a person – even though you may need to learn new skills and at times adjust your behaviour. At the core you are OK.

Our colleague had acknowledged her at many levels as coaching progressed, letting her know that her efforts were recognised. She had matched the client's own directness by clearly articulating when she thought the client was on-track and off-track in relation to her goals. She had, in other words, been championing her client. And because of this deep-down validation, this sometimes stroppy and defensive young woman had been willing to put herself on the line and commit to the challenging but ultimately rewarding process of coaching.

What do we mean by championing the client?

Championing clients is about defending and promoting them not to the outside world, but primarily to themselves. It is about cheering from the sidelines when you know how great an effort they are making – however small their achievements may seem to an outsider. Championing gets its strength from two things: from the fact that the coach is outside the client's situation and can see it from a more objective perspective and longer time frame and, above all, from the coach's belief in the client's ability to tackle what's needed in order to become what they have it in them to be. Championing is about being steadfast when the client is experiencing setbacks, helping them stick to their self-set agenda when they are exhausted, losing momentum or self-belief, and it is about modelling the importance of celebrating small steps rather than discounting minor achievements because there is still so much to do.

Championing rests on honesty. The 'encouragement' of a coach or commissioner who doesn't believe in the client's potential will come across as hollow and insincere – because it is. Equally, genuine and apparent faith in the client allows a championing coach to speak home truths when needed.

In her relationship with this client, our colleague had been demonstrating three key features of championing: building trust, acknowledging the client and keeping to the client's agenda.

Building trust

Trust is built from the very beginning of the coaching relationship. It's evidenced by designing the alliance and by agreeing to work to the client's agenda; it's shown through attentiveness and developed through making processes transparent; it is helped by setting clear boundaries and keeping to them; it's about two people being present, not just physically in attendance, whenever they meet. It's built by being committed and by taking the risk of expressing doubt or concern, if it arises, and doing it in a way that implies 'I'm raising this because it's getting in the way of something we both want – you achieving what you're capable of'.

Acknowledging the client

Acknowledgement means recognition at a fundamental level. Coming initially from the coach, it is not at all the same as praise. Too often praise tends to reinforce a sense of dependency. In this respect praise tends to be as bad as criticism and blame because it is perceived as coming from the coach's superior experience and expertise. At the extreme it can even feel patronising. 'Well done for trying' is what it may imply.

One reason for this paradoxical and unintended effect is that praise is usually keyed to externally observable behaviour. Acknowledgement, on the other hand, operates at a higher level: it offers a recognition of what the client's behaviour *means* and *costs*, and what it *says about them*. It's concerned with a higher frame of reference. This is why it can mean so much. 'It must have taken a lot for you to say that' tells the client that he is known and understood – and that the significance of his actions is truly recognised.

Sometimes it fulfils another function – it draws the client's attention to something they take for granted, when they think, 'doesn't everyone do that?' For example, a coach might identify one of her client's characteristic qualities that he thinks the client is overlooking or not appreciating, saying something like, 'Perhaps, as someone who naturally finds it easy to be conscientious, you don't realise why other people tend to rely on you so much?' This is how the supportive mirror that we talked of at the very beginning of the book works in practice. As the client's honest mirror, the coach reflects what is truly there. This is how it is: this is you, not just warts and all – but stars and all, too. Acknowledgement like this enhances trust – but it also encourages action.

Holding the client's agenda

Clients come to coaching with different kinds of agendas: their own and others' goals for them; short-term and long-term targets; plans for clearly defined external achievements and changes that they want to make, and more nebulous yet equally important goals such as 'feeling more fulfilled', 'doing something more worthwhile', 'being a better parent/partner', and so on.

While it's satisfying and worthwhile to tick off items on a to-do list, it's a vital part of the coach's job to help the client identify and then keep sight of this higher level agenda. For example, a good coach will not only register the deeper values and long-term goals that the client has expressed, but also be able to monitor when they are in danger of being eroded or obscured by the demands of the day. Then he might help the client back on her own track by saying something like, 'What impact might doing this have on your longer term goals?' or 'Are you really comfortable with that?' when he senses his client is compromising a belief that is important to her, or leaving herself out of the picture in order to fit in with others.

As coaching progresses, clients start to develop the habit of self-monitoring. For example, a junior manager we knew reflected, 'I wonder why that incident matters so much to me? Maybe it's because it's not just about making better presentations at work: no, it's more about feeling I have a right to be here in the world at all.'

What does championing the client achieve?

When you are taken this seriously, you begin to believe you are worth taking seriously. Everything conspires together to achieve this effect: the time that is set aside for you alone, the quality of the attention you receive from your coach that invites you to give yourself the same, the consistency of messages that simultaneously believe and expect you to be able to learn, grow and achieve. This is potent stuff. And it can affect you at every level, from helping you be more effective in your daily actions, through achieving a greater personal congruence with your deepest beliefs and values, to having a greater sense of belief and pride in being who you are.

Think of championing

- When you are setting the agenda you intend to be working on together.

- When your client is struggling or stuck.

- When you sense that she is despondent or experiencing setbacks.

- When you realise how much effort she is making – however small her apparent achievement at the time.

- When she isn't living up to her own potential.

- When she is making compromises at the level of beliefs and values or of identity.

- On days when there have been lots of setbacks. Ask what *has* been achieved?

However, ultimately the most powerful championing is self-championing. Championing yourself brings you two major benefits. First it is a powerful way of building self-confidence. Second, it helps you step outside situations that may be difficult, as it requires you to see them in the larger context of all that you bring. When you do this you see them from a different viewpoint. Even a few seconds looking at things from this alternative perspective can open up new ways of understanding and new possibilities for action.

How you can champion the client

- Don't encourage for encouragement's sake. Don't blame – and avoid praise that might be experienced as patronising. Be truthful to yourself and invite your client to do the same.

- Check out immediate or lower level agenda items against the client's higher order agenda by asking: 'What will that do for you?' and 'How will that serve you at a deeper, or higher, level?' and 'Does that conflict with what you really feel?'

- When acknowledging, use phrases that focus the client's attention on himself and his situation rather than allowing your opinion or views to obtrude: for example, 'You really put yourself on the line there' rather than 'I think you were courageous' or 'Well done.'

- Be prepared to challenge when you feel the client is not living according to her deepest beliefs or holding back from full commitment. Get her exploring why this is happening: there will be valid reasons, and holding the client to her agenda sometimes involves getting her both to acknowledge what is holding her back and to work with it, rather than to feel bad or condemn herself because of it.

MultiModal pointers

Logical Levels

Championing the client really targets issues of capability, beliefs, values and identity, even when it picks up on what they do and the way they do it. It's not the actions themselves but what lies behind them. That's why it can have such a powerful effect. It affirms – and stretches – the client as a whole.

Remedial-generative

By its very nature, championing is working towards generative ends. When you champion someone who is striving to master themselves more effectively, you are honouring effort and accomplishment that go way beyond mere filling in of gaps or catching up on limitations. The implications of stretching – and saluting – someone at such an important level are truly transforming. 'I found it really hard work to pass that maths exam,' said one client. 'I had to push myself to sit down with my books after a day at work. But my coach helped me to see that I was capable of more than I'd thought. Passing that exam has got me wondering. Maybe I could manage a part-time degree.'

Systemic implications

When you are perceived accurately, valued for what you truly are and encouraged to live up to your own agenda in the best way that you can, you are likely to feel more comfortable in your own skin. Even when things around you are tough or disappointing, you are less likely to be shaken at your core, so you will be more able to respond resourcefully and creatively. You may feel under pressure, but you are less likely to experience physical stress symptoms or disease. You are less likely to give yourself a hard time – in fact, your internal conversations may well become more confirming and encouraging. You are also less likely to compromise what truly matters to you, less likely to skimp or be half-hearted, and less likely to write off other people. You may find yourself more able to hold your corner and stand your ground, even if you used to find this difficult. Having been championed, you learn to self-champion and to champion others. There is a cascading effect, both at home and at work. You may find you are becoming a catalyst for others' self-development and self-actualisation. 'I find I'm reaching out to the younger fellows in the department now, instead of just letting them get on with things on their own or telling them off when they're not up to scratch,' said one junior manager. 'I try to give them the feeling I know where they're coming from and remember what it was like – that I believe they want to do well and that if they don't it's not because they're idle or stupid.'

Interpersonal-intra-psychic

Championing the client begins on the interpersonal dimension, with taking them seriously enough to expect the best of them in both senses. But it doesn't stop there: when you experience this kind of trust and the nurturing, you learn to give, and to expect, the same of yourself. This kind of faith in a person tends to raise the bar they have for themselves. As this attitude becomes habitual, you externalise it into your relations with those around you: friends, children and partners, colleagues ... It's like a wave that flows between inside and outside, between you and yourself, and between you and others. This is why this can be one of the most transformative processes in coaching.

Chapter Ten

Promote Integration

'We now know that the brain is built to linger as well as to rush ... We know that knowledge makes itself known through sensations, images, feelings and inklings, as well as through clear, conscious thoughts. Experiments tell us that just interacting with complex situations without trying to figure them out can deliver a quality of understanding that defies reason and articulation. Other studies have shown that confusion may be a vital precursor to the discovery of a good idea.'

Guy Claxton, *Hare Brain, Tortoise Mind,* Fourth Estate, 1998, page 203

Have you ever had the experience of attending an enjoyable, even inspirational, training event, learning a lot – and then finding that somehow you never quite put it into practice? When this happens the new learning and possibilities haven't been fully integrated by you. Sometimes they may even be in some conflict with things that are habitual or deeply important to you. They haven't become part of you. In other words, they haven't been integrated.

This is why promoting integration is *the* essential step that helps finalise any coaching, whether it's a one-off informal discussion that takes a coaching approach with a friend or colleague, or formal coaching lasting many months. Coaching is not just about what happens when it's actually occurring – it's about what happens *after-wards*. Indeed, most of the work from coaching takes place after the session, when understanding is being integrated and actioned.

What do we mean by promoting integration and how does it happen in practice?

The word 'integration' comes from the Latin '*integer*' meaning 'whole' or 'entire'. To integrate something is to make it part of the whole. All good coaching respects, and treats, the client as a whole – it's predicated upon the fundamental belief that you don't just work with one aspect of the client in isolation.

As the MultiModal model shows, every coaching session has potentially far-reaching implications, and in this chapter we use some of the distinctions in that model to show what integration can mean for the client and how coaching can promote it.

Elizabeth was a busy nursery assistant with two small children, a husband whose work often took him away and an elderly mother whose physical and mental health were both failing. She was having to assume responsibility for her mother, and went to see a life coach to think through whether to give up work and care for her mother at home, or sell her mother's house to pay for nursing home care. In the first session Elizabeth said she 'knew' that she should arrange nursing home care for her mother. But somehow she postponed making the necessary arrangements.

Elizabeth's coach was familiar with the Logical Levels model. The discrepancy between what Elizabeth 'knew she should do' and her failure to act on it suggested to him that she was in conflict at a high level – probably that of *beliefs and values*. So of course she had postponed taking any action (*behaviour*). When he asked her what stopped her acting on what she 'knew she should do', Elizabeth burst into tears. 'I would feel so guilty abandoning her after all she did for me when I was little,' she sobbed. The coach drew Elizabeth a diagram of the levels, explaining that they have to be aligned with each other if we are to feel comfortable with ourselves. 'Tell me which of these are out of line,' he said. Elizabeth drew her own version, which looked like this:

Identity
Beliefs and Values
Capability
     Behaviour
     Environment.

'I can't bring myself to put her in a home because I feel I owe her so much as a daughter,' she said. 'It's really my sense of identity that is involved here. And when push comes to shove, I'm a daughter first and foremost.'

'OK,' said her coach, 'But let's just begin by clarifying what values are most important for you, because it looks like unpacking this may give us the leverage we need to begin resolving things.'

'Well, I suppose that what's paramount is my mother's happiness.'

'And up to now you've been thinking she'd be happier living with you than being in a home?'

'Yes, of course.'

'Have you checked this out with your mother?' asked the coach.

'Well, no, actually I just assumed she'd hate being put away. I just assumed ...'

Elizabeth went home to have what she thought might be a difficult conversation with her mother. What actually happened really surprised her, because it turned out that her mother had been working on assumptions too! She found the noise and bustle of Elizabeth's children and their friends, and the disruption of coming and going, increasingly difficult to put up with. It tired her – and as she put it 'it makes me feel helpless and pointless. I can't join in – and I don't want to. But I thought you'd feel hurt if I said I'd rather live in a sheltered flat.' As Elizabeth said to her coach, 'I was in danger of doing the very thing I wanted to avoid – sacrificing my mother's happiness. But I was sacrificing it not to my wish to work, as I thought, but to my beliefs about what it meant to be a daughter.'

Using Logical Levels distinctions helped Elizabeth resolve much more than just a practical dilemma. It helped her realise exactly what kinds of issues were involved, and how easily actions, beliefs, values and identity can get tangled up. Her coach had helped her in a number of ways: he had got her to do some reality checking and helped her pinpoint what was really involved. But he'd also done more than this. By giving her the Logical Levels distinctions and encouraging her to use it for herself he had given her a new way of thinking which she could use in the future.

Such tools can help coaches and clients understand what's going on, find points of leverage and make the changes that are needed to restore or enhance integration.

What does promoting integration achieve?

When you help someone function in a more integrated way you help them feel better, think more clearly and act more authentically. And as a result they become more effective at managing themselves and their lives in general. With coaching, the kinds of integration we see most commonly involve integrating conscious cognitive planning with unconscious ease around change; integrating the present with that different proposed future; integrating new intra-psychic, within-the-self developments with new, external interpersonal behaviours; and integrating changes in one individual with the operations of the systems they are involved in.

As a by-product, people also become more resourceful, because they have learnt the habit of taking more factors into account and of seeking multiple solutions – and therefore they also become more confident. We know that the most effective managers are those who are able to use a variety of means to help them achieve their goals, adjusting their behaviour if necessary to accommodate changing circumstances. This also goes for management with a small 'm' – the management of your everyday life.

Some ways in which you can promote integration

- Asking 'How does that sit with you as a whole?' or 'Are you entirely comfortable with that?'

- Monitoring someone else's expression and posture for any changes that might indicate hesitation or lack of congruence.

- Paying attention to your own immediate 'gut feelings' when discussing plans or goals, and taking time to explore any discomfort you might feel.

- One of the most powerful ways of promoting integration is to integrate any proposed change into a person's future. So make the time to run a number of different future scenarios, from others' viewpoints as well as your own, to check strategies out for their larger systemic impact.

Think of promoting integration

- When you're learning something new or helping someone else with new learning.

- When agreed plans just aren't being followed through on.

- When complex issues or many viewpoints are involved.

- When someone is in a conflict situation.

- When you are approaching the end of any conversation about plans, goals or strategies.

- When you are coming towards the end of a course of coaching.

In these situations ask yourself and others what Logical Levels are involved. What systemic implications might there be? What generative possibilities? What intra-psychic as well as interpersonal concerns or effects?

Debbie's story

Debbie was in her mid-thirties with a degree in fashion. She had returned to the town where she had grown up, and used a legacy left by her uncle to start up a designer clothes shop. After a slow start, the business was succeeding. Her marriage, however, did not survive these upheavals, so she threw herself into work and into amateur dramatics, which gave her a ready-made social life. This was where she met Hugh, a divorced architect with two teenage daughters. They rapidly got into a passionate relationship, complicated by Hugh's jealous ex-wife.

Over the next nine months Debbie thought about breaking off the relationship several times. The 'sensible side' of her recognised that Hugh and his ex-wife still had many issues to sort out; she felt out of her depth in trying to be a substitute parent to the alternately dependent and difficult children; and she was taking so much time away from developing her business that sales were beginning to suffer. She really wanted to give the relationship a chance – and she also wanted to take her business forward.

Ever since she had started her own business, Debbie had belonged to a local group of business people which met regularly to network and give each other mutual support. Sometimes they invited external speakers and on one occasion the speaker was a coach. Debbie found his talk fascinating, and afterwards hired him so she could address the push-pull situation she felt she was in.

At their first coaching session, Debbie's coach asked her what she really wanted. 'I want to give my relationship time to build,' she said, 'but I also want to have enough time and energy to drive my business forward.' As they began to explore what was involved, Debbie came to realise that trying to juggle her work diary at the same time as 'being spontaneous' with Hugh just couldn't work. Moreover, she saw that by keeping this conflict within herself she was getting stressed and irritable and then taking it out on Hugh and the children.

Debbie's coach asked her to imagine a future when all these immediate problems had been solved. 'What kind of relationship will you be having with Hugh and the children then?' he asked. 'One in which we can trust each other because we know we're on the same team. One where we can talk things through together and solve them together,' said Debbie immediately. 'So what's to stop you doing that right now?'

There was a long pause. 'Well, nothing, I suppose,' replied Debbie. 'I've just got to get my courage up and talk with them. I guess I've been afraid of taking that risk, in case they wouldn't take my life and my needs seriously – but if they won't, or can't, the bottom line really is that this relationship can't go forward anyway. That would be pretty hard to take – but maybe it's better to find that out now rather than putting it off and hoping.'

After thinking things through for a couple of days, Debbie decided to raise the issue at a family lunch the next weekend. Later, she reported to her coach that the lunch had had its awkward moments, but that she really did feel the four of them had focused on what was concerning her. 'The kids said they had enjoyed the things we've done together – but they certainly hadn't realised how much is involved in developing a business. Hugh's daughter, Lisa, was really interested in my buying trips and asked if I'd let her do her work experience week with me in the summer. And Hugh has bought a family calendar so we can all put our dates and plans on it. It's too soon to tell long term what will happen, but I feel we've made a start at being a team ... you know, I think I'd love it if we became a family.'

Debbie had originally come for coaching because she felt she couldn't manage two sets of things she wanted to do (*behaviour*) – develop her relationship with Hugh and his children and continue to take her business forward. Both involved building her skills and managing her time and her diary (*capability*). But what really worried her deep down was whether she could maintain her sense of herself as a businesswoman while at the same time becoming a partner and an active carer for Hugh's children (issues of *values and identity*).

Debbie had started coaching to find a way out of a situation (*a remedial brief*). But now she was beginning to realise that much more was at stake. The short-term highs of the relationship and of her burgeoning business were not enough. She wanted a real future and started thinking *generatively* about how her life could be. She was already aware that any decisions she might make would have repercussions, not just for Hugh and herself, but also for the children (*systemic concerns*). She had not, however, allowed herself to recognise that there was another very important systemic effect that this relationship was having on her: the excitement of the start of the relationship had soon been offset by her feelings of conflict and irritability. This *intra-psychic* stress was in danger of being played out *interpersonally*. Left unchecked this could become a *reinforcing feedback loop* with potentially disastrous consequences.

The work that Debbie and her coach did together created a *balancing feedback loop*. As Debbie reframed her feelings of conflict as an issue which she and her new 'family' might be able to manage together, she initiated a new way of being with them which laid the foundation for the family 'team' she had dreamed of. Talking through the complex issues involved with Hugh and his children began to give Debbie not only a way through her immediate dilemma, but also a way of engaging which 'will hopefully be with us as a tool for the rest of our lives'.

Diccon's story

Diccon was a middle manager in a large international corporation. His work was good enough – in fact, he compared well with many of his peers. But his manager felt that he could perform even better 'if his heart was in it'. Joan from HR agreed, and felt that Diccon – and the firm – might benefit from him having some coaching. Although the offer took him by surprise, Diccon readily accepted it. 'If I'm honest with myself I think Joan and my manager are right,' he said. 'I can do this work easily, and I quite enjoy it – but it doesn't really engage me. Work pays the mortgage and that's about it.'

As Diccon and his coach began to discuss this rather nebulous issue it became clear that it was not one of ability: Diccon had plenty of that. Nonetheless, there was a dislocation somewhere: in his heart of hearts Diccon didn't see himself as a middle manager in a big firm, and he didn't believe that working there long term – even if he did well and obtained promotion – would significantly express the person he really was.

Diccon's coach asked him to do two things: find stories of people that really interested him, and ask at least ten people who he knew – friends, family members and colleagues – to write a single paragraph describing the Diccon they knew. When he reported back he said, 'All the people whose lives really grabbed my attention had a passion which they made time for. They seemed really alive. That's how I want to be – but I don't have a passion like that in my life and I can't think how I'd get one. So that made me feel even more depressed. But on the positive side, when I started to get back those mini-profiles, I realised that people value me for *how* I do things, not *what* I do. I didn't think of myself as someone who could put people at their ease, or make a party go with a swing, or be fun to go on holiday with, or listen sympathetically, or help people learn. Yet those were all things people said about me. I'm not in the wrong business, not even in the wrong firm – just in the wrong job. I'm a people person really. There's an enthusiast in me looking for something to be enthusiastic about.'

It wasn't long before Diccon found his answer. He asked his line manager if he could spend some time mentoring younger people in the department. The feedback was very positive. Over the next few years his firm sent him on a number of short courses, and eventually gave him the time and financial support he needed to take a professional HR qualification. He still works for the same company but in a very different capacity.

SECTION 3: Coaching – the Larger Issues

Overview: Life Issues

> One of the most important questions that a coach can ask is, 'What did you learn about yourself?'

Thomas G. Crane, *The Heart of Coaching*, FTA Press, 2002, page 117

It has been said that despite the endless stream of stories over many centuries there is really only a small number of basic plots in literature. In the same way, you could say there are just a small number of core issues in life, although the forms they take are endlessly varied. For each person, at different times, one or other of these may become more pressing; but coaching of any kind addressing almost any specific content will come up against them at some time. Rather than attempting a definitive list of core issues – that's another book! – we want to show how engaging with these greater issues enriches, invigorates and informs all coaching. We'll also offer some ways in which you can develop the alertness that makes this possible.

Life issues: a wider awareness in coaching

When some friends bought their first house the vendors told them that the plaster on the kitchen wall had recently fallen away and been repaired. Some years later the same thing began to happen again, and again it was repaired. Later again, when the telltale signs came back, they decided that this time the whole wall, not just a patch, should be done. When the builder stripped off the whole area, he found rising damp, penetrating damp and some patches of dry rot in an old door frame that had been plastered over and hidden many years previously. Tinkering with the surface had just masked the underlying issues – so of course they recurred.

Why is it useful to have a wider awareness in coaching? Surely if someone brings a specific problem – for example changing jobs, dealing with the boss more effectively, improving performance in sport, or balancing time at work and time for life outside it – it's enough to address that? Of course, coaching can and does help people with specific problems; but it's our experience that even in these terms they gain more if their immediate need is approached in a wider context. The issues that bring people into coaching are usually both symptomatic and reflective of wider issues, just as they are in other areas of life.

Becoming aware of wider life issues does *not* mean that you have to set aside the initial goals you had for coaching. Rather, it allows you to put specific or immediate needs within a broader context. Learning to 'place' presenting issues in this way means that – rather like the process of checking for alignment across the Logical Levels – you can often achieve much more than you first expected. Maybe you'll sort out not just the current decision you need to make, or help an employee with a difficulty at work, but also find out something about how you go about making decisions in general, what your values really are deep down inside or just why this colleague keeps coming up against this kind of problem.

This wider awareness can create a lot of leverage and a big pay-off. A runner seeking to improve her times made huge progress when her coach helped her with underlying issues of personal confidence; a new manager having difficulties with staff found it much easier to be clear and effective in managing them once she recognised that her childhood learning that girls are expected to rely mainly on charm to influence others meant that she was either too 'soft' or too manipulative. A new client in a first session describing his immediate problem was asked, 'Does this kind of issue arise anywhere else in your life?' There was a moment's pause, then a deep sigh. 'Aah ... yes, it does.' And he rattled off a string of examples, both personal and professional. The coach's question, even at this opening stage of their work, shifted it from a narrowly defined single remedial focus to a wider consideration of a life issue. This opened up the possibility that their work could go beyond remedial patching to a generative reconfiguring of the beliefs and attitudes that were driving a whole raft of behaviours in different contexts.

There's another advantage, too. When you pick up and begin to address an underlying life issue, its very pervasiveness means that the changes and improvements you make will cascade through a number of areas, not just the one that led to coaching in the first place. The runner improved her times – and started having a romantic relationship. The new manager took control of her business – and got on better with her son. The client who had the 'Aah!' moment in his very first session went on to find that his subsequent sessions brought benefits in his work, his family life and his sporting activities, even though none of these had been specifically targeted in his coaching.

While in one way it's a serious business to engage with yourself and others at this level, it doesn't have to be heavy, earnest or driven. Quite the reverse in fact – your sense of relief and rightness when things 'click into place' can actually make you feel as though a weight has been lifted. You'll probably become more light-hearted. You may well be able to laugh at yourself and tease others caught up in the old pattern. A trainer we knew was irked by a colleague who tended to 'take over'. When he addressed his part in allowing this to happen, the next time his colleague began to muscle in he found himself quite naturally joking, 'Oi! Whose session is this?'

What does being alert actually involve?

Being alert is not the same as being vigilant. Ian's dog can be truly relaxed – yet from time to time an ear will orientate itself in the direction of an unexpected sound, and when he hears the sound of Ian's car returning he'll recognise it before anyone else does and jump up. There's no anxiety or stress in this – he's just receptive and continually monitoring his environment.

By contrast, 'the price of freedom is eternal vigilance.' Without that vigilance, that which is so precious is eroded and then lost. Being vigilant can be quite stressful. It's often a state of 'watching out for' mostly something unpleasant or dangerous. The hero of J.K. Jerome's *Three Men in a Boat*, feeling off-colour, began reading the medical dictionary. The more he read, the more he was astonished to realise that he was currently experiencing each set of symptoms – a phenomenon also well known among medical students. In the end, he was convinced he had every disease in the book, apart from housemaid's knee. At its extreme, vigilance takes us beyond even hypochondria to paranoia – both states in which people personalise what's going on inside or around them and interpret it for the worst.

What is the difference between this kind of vigilance and the alertness we are recommending? Such vigilance is fearful, self-referring and at times self-obsessed. It also lacks any perspective. Many years ago one of our clients was undergoing a period of extreme personal stress. She had also, coincidentally, suffered a small cut. Waking one morning with a stiff neck and aching jaw, she became convinced that she had tetanus. As she tells it, it was only when she found herself driving at high speed and with extreme skill to see the doctor that she told herself that, given her driving ability, the one thing she certainly *hadn't* got was tetanus! But, as she went on to recognise, she was certainly immobilised and feeling trapped by her situation.

The contrast between what our client believed and what she was actually able to do shifted her into a *neutral place* where she could assess the situation more objectively and without the obsessive anxiety and fear that she had been feeling. Through her coaching she'd become aware that quite often her body would send her 'messages' that mirrored metaphorically what was going on in her mind: in this case, her body was telling her in no uncertain terms that she was 'stuck and trapped'. This gave her a wider awareness of an issue in her life.

The kind of awareness we are talking about, then, is characterised by a certain easing out. It's like being able to step outside yourself and see what is going on without judgement and without the distraction of strong emotion. 'Hey, so that's what's going on, then ...', you may say to yourself. 'So that's what this is all about.' You've moved from a singular perspective to a multiple one, in which you are simultaneously subject and object of your own awareness, with the possibility of a very fruitful dialogue between them. You've moved from focusing on the specifics to an awareness of overall pattern and meaning. You've moved from information through knowledge to a personal wisdom.

Developing your alertness

Developing this kind of alertness is essentially about two things: becoming more receptive and getting into the habit of asking bigger questions. It's a kind of personal evolution. If you are urgently focused on a task or a need you will tend to filter out any information that doesn't seem to relate to it. It's a bit like looking at a stereogram. (A stereogram is a two-dimensional image that has a three-dimensional image hidden within it, which can only be seen when you defocus.) Taking the pattern at surface value can blind you in one way so you don't discern what's embedded; looking too intently can blind you in another way. The trick is simply to look with soft eyes and allow what's present to emerge and come into focus.

For this to occur, it helps to be in an enquiring, playful yet attentive state of mind – just the mind-set that characterises good coaching. Being alert is all about being open. It's about a willingness to receive what's available, and to allow multiple possible meanings rather than run them through preconceived filters. It's also about coming to know what your personal filters are, and learning to compensate for the bias they produce.

So you notice the pattern, and you observe its effects. Then you ask yourself, 'are these the effects I want?' In the case of ineffective patterns, your answer is likely to be 'no'. But once you have identified the pattern, you can begin to deconstruct it. You can ask yourself questions like:

- What's going on here?

- What is this an example of?

- What's the larger issue here?

- Is there a repeated sequence of actions, thoughts or feelings (or all three)?

- Is there a trigger?

- What are the effects?

- Where are the moments when I have a choice to do something different?

- What would I want to have happen instead?

- What would be the smallest difference I could make that would begin to interrupt – even derail – this pattern?

Asking questions like these is a potent way of enriching your understanding and your relationship with yourself. You will become aware of different perspectives you might take and so have more choice. You may also find you have rather more useful internal conversations with yourself.

When you do this, you're creating a space for yourself, which is the very opposite of rushing into activity. One of our clients who worked as a sales trader in an international bank was referred for coaching because he tended to become frustrated and lose his temper under pressure. After only a short time of coaching he said that the first major benefit he had gained was that he'd learnt to create a 'breathing space' at the beginning of each day before plunging into its urgent tasks and demands. Taking that time – even if he was under such pressure that it could only be a few minutes – meant that he could think about priorities and how he was going to manage himself: he could plot his chosen course and steer it, rather than being blown and battered hither and yon by the day's events. Similarly, we know a busy woman who found that taking space like this for herself each day after her children had gone to bed meant that she had time to reflect and refresh herself. In turn this meant she was able to enjoy time with her partner more and be less harried the day after.

Good coaching helps to create this spacious and neutral awareness. So-so coaching may collude with the client's wish to 'do something' and end up encouraging a flight into action – on the dubious grounds that coaching is about making changes and doing something different. Doing something is not necessarily the same as changing something, or improving something – activity is no substitute for purpose and vision.

We consider being able to create this more spacious awareness a useful litmus test for quality in coaching. So often it seems to be what promotes generative systemic change. There are three chapters in this section. In each of these we'll be exploring a different area where it can make such a crucial difference.

Working with key life issues

> *A successful coaching relationship is always a story of transformation, not just of higher levels of performance. It's a story that takes people beyond their immediate passion and pride and helps them come to grips with the fact that to reach what is really possible and achievable for them, they must be willing to fundamentally question who they are, what they do, and why they do it.*

Robert Hargrove, *Masterful Coaching*, Jossey-Bass/Pfeiffer, 2003, page 103

Suppose you have given yourself some time, found a kind of neutral space inside yourself and are cultivating an engaged relationship with yourself while having a more emotionally detached perspective on yourself. How are you going to use this more spacious awareness to best effect? We have found that there is a lot of mileage to be had in asking three questions. In our experience clients who have been asked these questions in coaching soon begin to ask them of themselves.

We want to look at these three key questions and explore the leverage they can give you. One way to think of them is as themes that underlie *all* coaching topics, whether your coaching is about life balance, work issues or personal life changes and choices. They are:

1. What am I voting for?

2. How can I best manage myself?

3. What's my purpose?

What are you voting for?

Everything you do involves – at least potentially – *not* doing something else. As a client's angry daughter told her when she prevaricated yet again, 'If you keep on not making that decision you're actually making a decision by *not* doing anything!'

Our colleague Jan Elfline developed a very useful analogy for highlighting the fact that we're continually making choices and in doing so she helped people to own them and make more effective choices about them. She likens our daily decisions to voting. Using her analogy of casting a vote helps clarify what's really going on. If, like one of our business clients, you want to lose weight but keep on eating out 'because entertaining is part of the job', and if you don't change how and what you eat, you're voting for being overweight. Do it consistently over time and you're also voting for potential ill health and maybe diet-related illnesses.

If your finances are tight but you buy lots of things in the sales because they're so cheap, you may be voting for continued stress and anxiety. Do this enough over time and you're voting for never being able to provide properly for your old age. Actions have consequences – even little actions. Every action, however small, casts a vote. So do many thoughts: each time you expect the worst you engrain a pattern of pessimism, or helplessness, or resentment.

However, you can start to make changes at any time, once you become aware of your voting pattern and where it's taking you. Your next meal, for instance, can be the beginning of feeding yourself what your body wants and needs rather than what you've got used to. If you don't buy that 'bargain' you've saved even more. If you say 'no' this once, maybe you've made a dent in the old pattern of your relationship with your relatives.

Often, people think that change has to be major: we invite you to consider the opposite – that a big change can be achieved through the cumulative effect of repeated 'voting'. Every day consists of making decisions, many of them quite small. Considered cumulatively, how do yours stack up? What are you voting for in terms of your expenditure of those three essentials *time*, *money* and *energy*? For example, what about that acquaintance you keep on meeting for old times' sake, but who seems to leave you feeling drained and depressed after each meeting. Are you investing your energy wisely in continuing to keep the relationship going? Our point is not that any one particular expenditure is inherently 'better' or 'worse', but rather that by examining your personal voting record you can decide whether you are voting for the values and outcomes that you truly want, or not. And if not, you have the power to do something about it, day by day and vote by vote.

Jot down the values you hold dear. You can include anything that matters to you, from creativity to family life right through to world peace. Now look at your voting patterns – the way you spend your time, money and energy – in relation to the values you listed. Do they match up? If not, what are you really voting for? If that isn't how you want it, where can you begin to make changes?

People are often critical of politicians: they'll contrast their fine words against what they actually do. At other times they're accused of double-speak or hypocrisy. But we have found it very fruitful to explore for ourselves and with our clients just how authentic *we* are being in our own lives. So you might therefore want to ask yourself 'how's my own voting record?' Are you in danger of speaking with a forked tongue to yourself and making promises you don't deliver? Are you perhaps even trying to placate different constituencies within yourself – a bit of you, for example, may be wanting to give your family a good standard of living by working the insane hours that earn you a good salary, while another bit of you could be wanting to spend time enjoying some kind of home life.

How can you best manage yourself?

When you know what your values are and what you really want out of your life you can compare them to your behaviour and begin to assess how effective you are at managing yourself in relation to them. Values and goals may provide the drive and the purpose. But those voting patterns you identified tell you *how* you're currently managing yourself, your behaviour and your habits. The question is, do these support you in achieving what you say matters to you?

There's another aspect to self-management, too, which is recognising your patterns. We all have strengths and weaknesses. However, strengths aren't always the unalloyed bonus they may seem: so often they can be our greatest potential weaknesses – if only because we tend to play to them too often. That means we're always in danger of doing rather too much of what we're good at instead of developing a broader range of skills and sympathies.

Suppose you are good at being assertive. Are you equally good at knowing when to compromise or give way? Every strength – employed in the wrong place or at the wrong time – can also be a limitation. We have come across a number of ex-army personnel now working in management. They're great at discipline, leadership, teamwork and serving the ethics of the organisations they belong to. But these same qualities can also make it harder for them to let themselves or others off the hook, even when it's appropriate, or to respond easily when emotions are involved. If they got serious about learning to be more human they would actually become better leaders. Then they wouldn't be facing the frustration of finding promotion to senior levels consistently eluding them.

Consider the converse, too. What strengths may lie dormant in your weaknesses? Rather than taking a remedial view of weaknesses, it helps to consider them as the flip side of a related strength. Find it difficult to plan ahead? Maybe it's the flip side of being able to get really immersed in what you're doing right now. Many times we've asked clients to list their weaknesses and then find the gold in them. Invariably, this is a revelation and changes their sense of self. So this can therefore be an identity level intervention that frees people up to see themselves differently.

Managing yourself, just like managing others, is about knowing who you are and how you tick. Really good coaching builds this muscle so that ultimately self-management becomes an act of self-leadership.

What's your purpose?

Being productive is not the same as having a purpose. Nor is being creative. When you start asking what your purpose is you are definitely becoming alert to wider issues. You're moving into the big questions, like 'why am I here?', 'what do I want my life to have been about?'

These are questions at the very highest Logical Level: they reach *beyond identity*. They raise questions of meaning and of mission, and can take you into the dimension of spirit and the spiritual. For most people, thinking of yourself and your life in this way helps you set the rest of your concerns in a much more meaningful context.

You can get there by a number of routes – and one is coaching. When Ian is coaching people, he sometimes asks them: 'What do you want your legacy to be – (to your family, your organisation, even the world)?' Most people find this way of thinking about themselves unfamiliar and even daunting. They seem to think they'll only leave a legacy if they're in some way special or outstanding. Fine if you're Mother Teresa, or Ghandi, or Bill Gates or Winston Churchill. But this really isn't true. Recently, some Indian friends were on a skiing holiday with their children. While out the kids encountered some other children, who taunted them by calling them 'niggers'. Those children were not born with that social attitude. In this case it was their parents' prejudices coming out. So those parents have therefore sent their fear and their hatred into the future. That, too, is a legacy.

In a sense we cannot *not* leave a legacy because we will influence others for good or ill. So what do you want your legacy to be? If you dare to ask yourself this kind of question it will rapidly become clear whether what you're doing now is taking you in the right direction or not. It's not about achievements. It's not about being outstandingly gifted. It *is* about being uniquely and specially *yourself*. Once you know what this means for you at this time in your life, you're on the way to identifying your purpose. You can come to know what serves it, what fits with it, and what detracts or distracts from it. In this way you begin to feel and to own what you're here for. And perhaps the biggest pay-off of all is that getting clear about what you want your legacy to be invariably impacts what you choose to do right now and from hereon in.

Becoming alert to life issues and learning to work with them is a litmus test of good coaching. It's one of the things that differentiate the journeyman coach from the master craftsman. If you're a client, it's one of the things that will help you most and take you furthest because it's transformative. And as you embody it in your life it may also become part of your legacy to others.

Chapter Eleven

Being Impeccable

> *Imagine a world where people are willing to truly listen not only to the words but to everything behind the words. Imagine a world in which you could hear and receive the hard truth and find the learning in the truth instead of diving for your defenses. What if we held out for each other and our children the biggest picture possible of what they could be instead of pointing out their limitations.*
>
> *... It would be a world where we hold each other to account for who we are and what we say we will do. In this world we are as committed to the truth about ourselves as we are to the truth we tell to others.*
>
> Laura Whitworth, Henry Kimsey-House and Phil Sandahl, *Co-Active Coaching*,
> Davies-Black Publishing, 1998, pages 175–6

Our experience tells us that when a commissioner, coach and client approach their work in this spirit, and endeavour to treat each other in these ways, their achievements are infinitely greater and often have wider-reaching systemic repercussions. This is what we mean when we talk about 'being impeccable' – a way of relating to oneself and others that includes but goes far beyond letter-of-the-law prescriptions about best professional practice.

Being impeccable is different from being punctilious. Yes, it's important to be meticulous and consistent – but it's more important that you are genuine. Developing expertise is valuable – but you really must also care, in the case of the coach, about your clients and the process known as coaching. Because you care you'll always be seeking to go beyond what you have accomplished to date. You will have high standards for yourself and what you deliver. One way these will show up is in your striving to walk your talk in your own life. Being impeccable in your behaviour usually comes from working according to the spirit of a wider set of beliefs and standards. This is what inspires you and makes you aspire to be more.

Being impeccable in coaching is enacted in daily behaviour. If you value someone else's uniqueness, you respect it in the way you behave towards them – and in how you expect them to behave towards you in return. And it's not just coaches who can model this in the way they behave. We know one experienced commissioner of coaching, for example, called Tom, who makes a point of shaping coaches' and clients' expectations through his use of transparency. To take just one example, he asked a coach and client to attend an initial meeting. The aim was to clarify a fairly tight brief, inform the coach, summarise the issues to be addressed and flag some possible problems that might arise. Tom made it clear that the client had the freedom to decide whether she felt able to work with this potential coach. There were no hidden items, no behind-the-scenes confidential briefings. All three parties agreed there and then a 'package' that would be appropriate if coaching went ahead, covering the probable number of sessions and their length and timing. The client agreed to say yes or no within 48 hours. If her answer was no, other coaches would be available. For Tom it's important that he can successfully match clients and coaches and get really good results. Being upfront in this way enables him to consistently achieve this.

Why does being impeccable matter?

Being impeccable is part of the basic fabric of coaching – the underlying warp and weft that give substance to its surface texture and pattern. In this chapter we want to show how you can realistically become impeccable in your dealings with yourself and others without being superhuman or self-denying. In fact, in our experience working impeccably actually *frees* you to be more responsive and more real – especially in coaching. It means being both generous and rigorous in addressing things as they are. It also means being alert to opportunities to clarify and work towards your desired goals.

Being impeccable in a coaching relationship involves being consistent – but consistency can mean many things. Coaching consistency requires clear and coherent values, and applying high standards in daily practice. Consistency across all Logical Levels ensures that you are at one with yourself; consistency in process and flow helps build long-lasting habits of effectiveness; and as coaching progresses there's a growing consistency between the model of enquiry and interacting that the coach offers the client and the way the client engages with himself. From the outset, a good coach will implicitly and explicitly model this through her behaviour and her words, and she will encourage her client to keep this important framework in mind as he addresses the immediate issues or goals that bring him to coaching. She may ask him to name the values he holds dear; she will alert him when he seems likely to compromise these values; she will invite him to support his values through the regular patterns and structures of his daily life and she will encourage him to expect high standards of himself and of others.

Being impeccable isn't the same as being perfect

Although we can't be perfect, we *can* be impeccable. Being impeccable isn't the same as being perfect. Perfectionism tends to produce intolerance, both of others and of oneself. The unrealistic expectations it creates are anything but impeccable – they lead to blaming and shaming and holding grudges. Being impeccable means having high standards and being able to forgive yourself and others for honest errors.

▶ **Being impeccable means maintaining your own standards while accepting the challenge to be compassionate.** A potential client arranged to telephone a coach to discuss what she wanted to gain from coaching and to make initial arrangements. She knew she had many things on her plate and that she was finding it difficult to juggle them. She was also aware that she had always had problems in staying focused. In this first phone call, not surprisingly, she kept wandering from the agreed task of finding a focus for coaching and agreeing practicalities. While the coach remained understanding and non-judgemental, he brought her back to the point each time she went off-track and reminded her of the call's purpose. After several such reminders, she began to catch herself as she diverged – 'I've done it again, haven't I?' Her coaching had begun.

▶ **Being impeccable means recognising and addressing your own issues rather than projecting them onto others.** The less sorted out your issues are, the greater the danger of them contaminating your responses to others. You might be a coach, yet in your personal life you still wish you'd gotten even with so and so. Along comes a client in a similar situation. Will you encourage him to do what you still ache to do – or will you be able to engage with *his* experience and support him in finding *his* own best course of action?

You are commissioning coaching for a team member, and were really impressed by the way a previous coach addressed 'the same problem' last year with another colleague. It would be so easy to brief the potential coach as though the team member, the situation and the coaching approach were all the same. Or will you rein your-self in, recognising that your own perspective may limit what can be achieved? You're a client, and you find that when your coach suggests a task you react to them just like you used to react to your mother: in fact, you realise that was why you didn't do the tasks you'd agreed from your last session. Will you keep quiet about this, try to force yourself to do them this week – or will you talk about what's really been going on?

Being impeccable means caring enough to do your own psychic and emotional spring-cleaning so you are less at the mercy of forces like these. It means recognising any similarity to your own personal experience, resisting the temptation to advise or prescribe, and bringing the focus back onto the other person – be they your child, a subordinate or your client – in a search for *their* resources and *their* solutions.

▶ **Being impeccable means you commit to life-long learning because you know how limited your knowledge is and you care enough to want to understand more.** It was once said that '30 years' experience' could merely mean one year's experience repeated 30 times. By contrast, outstanding coaches seek out new learning, test theories and practices, and take the risk of operating at the edge of their existing competence. In this way they offer their clients a powerful model of what it means to be a continuing learner. Every client calls for a subtly different approach – because every client is unique. This is part of the buzz for the coach, and at the same time it carries a powerful message to the client. He is not being put through a routine process, or straightjacketed to fit a preordained model, however successful it may have been in the past. He exists in his own right and is being met on his own terms.

▶ **Being impeccable means you care enough to confront the truth even if it's uncomfortable.** When a client doesn't challenge a statement that doesn't 'fit', when a coach lets something significant slip by, when a commissioner doesn't clarify a contractual boundary, when one slips, the message is that it's OK to make do – and even that it's OK to settle for second best.

Maybe it would have been 'easier' for the coach not to point out when the new client was wandering off the point. But by challenging the client, the coach was effectively saying 'I take you and your goals seriously – so let's begin as we mean to go on, by working directly and cooperatively in a way that serves you and them.'

Would it be easier for a client whose coach has made a suggestion about what might be happening, or about a task the client might do, to 'accept' it even if it doesn't seem correct, or useful or manageable, mentally reserving the right to discard it or 'forget' to do it? Or would it be better to say, 'You know, I'm not sure it's really like that' or 'That feels too much of a challenge right now'?

Where a coach doesn't seem to have achieved much with a client, would it be easier for a commissioner just to quietly drop the coach from his list and use other coaches in future? Or would it be more beneficial – as well as more honest – to discuss the case with the coach and work out why it has seemed unsatisfactory? Has the progress been slow or just in unexpected directions? And if little progress has been made, how come? And what is there to learn for the future? Being impeccable means you pluck up your courage to speak your truth in such moments.

▶ **Being impeccable means you understand the importance of timing and respect it.** In learning of any kind, timing is critical. Teachers used to talk about 'reading readiness' to describe that moment when a child becomes able to put together a range of complex, consciously learnt skills and suddenly cross the threshold and become a reader. In our adult lives we may also experience getting ready or building up to making a change. Good coaches both register and encourage such readiness. Conversely, they're also aware when a client is not ready to understand, to act on something learnt or to take a risk. Skilful coaching is about knowing when to allow someone a while in their comfort zone and when to encourage a stretch.

Such knowledge is based not on an unvarying rule but on observation of *this* situation and *this* client. It comes from registering a person's usual pattern of responses and then noticing those slight variations that indicate doubt or delight, anxiety or excitement, discomfort or ease.

Living by your rules

Being impeccable is about what you *do*. It's found in all walks of life, in all cultures and all civilisations – as, of course, is its opposite. It's about consistently living your values every day. To do that you need to check in with yourself and track what is really going on inside you. Sometimes this may not be so comfortable. A skilled professional we knew said he was feeling down and unsure about where he wanted to go in his life, and what he wanted to be doing. It was important that he – and his coach – honour these feelings of stagnation and frustration. Only then could he start to create the space in his life to allow new possibilities to seed and to grow.

Being impeccable means honouring the wisdom of others while not belittling your own. It means learning to take your ideas and insights seriously rather than believing or hoping that someone else – your coach, say – will have the answer.

For a coach, it means being willing to draw upon all you have learnt from teachers, colleagues and past clients, yet being willing to trust your own instinctive responses when they take you in a different direction.

To be impeccable you'll probably need to be reasonably internally coherent. This has its own pay-offs. One of the characteristics of effective people is that they are at one with themselves: this means that they are comfortable in their skins and with their own mental processing – logical and intuitive, conscious and unconscious. They are mostly congruent with themselves across all the Logical Levels, recognise when something is 'out', and seek both to know why and to bring themselves back into harmony again.

Being impeccable isn't always easy – but in the long run it's *easier* because it allows you to be human without guilt or shame. It's the basis of honest contracting in every kind of relationship, including the one you have with yourself. You know in your heart of hearts when you are letting yourself down, or fudging an issue. For some it starts on the outside: as you cease doing this with others it makes you wonder why you should do it with yourself. For others it starts on the inside: when you behave towards yourself impeccably it's so much easier to extend that to those around you. Either way it makes us wonder if it's ever worth being less than impeccable – it's just enlightened self-interest.

Being impeccable is at the very core of coaching. It isn't as difficult – or as absolute – as it may sound, and it really delivers high quality to every relationship you're engaged in. Being impeccable will certainly ensure that you get the most out of coaching. But beyond that it will help you get the most out of being alive.

Chapter Twelve

Becoming Generative

> *Companies are searching for undiscovered reserves of value. Human nature is one of those last, vast reserves of value. If they are to increase their value, companies know they must tap these reserves. In the past they have tried to access the power of human nature by containing it and perfecting it, just as mankind has done with the other forces of nature. We now know why this cannot work: the power of human nature is that, unlike other forces of nature, it is not uniform. Instead its power lies in its idiosyncrasy, in the fact that each human's nature is different. If companies want to use this power, they must find a mechanism to unleash each human's nature, not contain it. You ... are the best mechanism they have.*

> Marcus Buckingham and Curt Coffman, *First, Break all the Rules*, Free Press Business, 2001, page 242

To generate is to evolve something or to bring it newly into existence. Being generative means having what it takes to bring something forth – and then doing so. Ultimately, this usually involves some kind of innovation.

One dimension of the MultiModal template is the continuum that runs from coaching that is remedial to coaching that is generative. If working remedially is to cover your back, to catch up, or to plug the holes of your limitations, working generatively is to go beyond the everyday and the familiar, to get into the zone, to stretch, strive and bring forth. Where remedial work tends to be located towards the safety end of the continuum of human motivation, generative work is right up there on the growth end. Yet being generative embraces more than this: it's an attitude, a state of mind, an ability to meet experience with all your resources on tap but without preconceptions or preconditions as to how they should be applied. This chapter is about the role coaching can play in helping people do this, both for themselves and for others. In this sense, and in our experience, coaching in itself can be a supremely generative process.

Being generative is more than just being productive or even creative. Coaching assumes that people have both the capacity and the wish to be productive. So often, though, in the workplace 'productive' is used in the very limited – and often limiting – sense of doing more. When we use the words 'productive', or 'productivity', we are often referring to measures of volume, quantity or speed. Changing any of these can be useful outcomes of coaching, but they are not necessarily generative. Concepts and actions that are generative do not leave the world quite as they found it, whether that world is the world of the organisation, the informal network, the world of ideas or the interior world of the individual. Being generative *makes a difference.*

One way it can do this is by stirring up the existing pieces of experience and leaving them in a different relationship to each other. It makes new connections. Generative interventions and inventions are not necessarily dramatic in themselves, but they have far-reaching results. Take the hovercraft. All its components existed previously, yet the concept of having a sea-going vehicle create its own contained cushion of air to provide a relatively frictionless interface with the sea was both generative and innovative. The idea took what was already available, went beyond it and spawned a whole new way of thinking.

Being generative can also manifest as entrepreneurism – and not just in business. We know of a very large school that had a very small drama department, with two staff out of a total of over 90. Drama departments are always in need of funds. So the head of department bought snacks wholesale, sold them to pupils at breaks and made his department a substantial profit. First he was able to buy the extra equipment; later his profits were sufficient to buy the school a new minibus. And a lot of pupils saw how one individual's initiative can have an impact.

Truly generative effects can also come about through 'small' interventions. One of our clients, a busy senior executive, had a regular 40-minute train journey to work. Out of the available 80 minutes per day, he set aside 20 to study a new language. Such a little time – yet, multiplied ... From French he progressed to German, and then Greek. His 'small' intervention had truly generative effects, giving him access to enormous horizons opening up what he called 'whole new worlds'.

Learning, caring, guiding, teaching, producing and creating are all aspects of being generative and where people feel these are significantly lacking, whether at work or at home, they are likely in consequence to feel empty, unfulfilled, or without meaning and purpose. It's for this reason that we believe 'generativity' relates as much to states of *being* as it does to acts of *doing*. Once fundamental issues like this have been addressed, the client is able to look forward, to explore and to discover more of what she can become. This is generative work at a personal level. As she becomes more able to manage herself and her impact on her world, the client is also more able to be generative systemically and at the level of ideas. This may well mean that she also becomes, in her own and others' eyes, more productive.

In this chapter we explore what becoming generative can actually involve and what, specifically, it can deliver.

The coaching space

If you are to become generative in your work and other aspects of your life, you need space. Ever been too busy to really achieve anything? You've been running around, feeling under pressure, yet have so little to show for it? Or maybe you've been turning out a lot, but wonder if it's really worth much after all? The likelihood is that you haven't had the space to reflect or to prioritise – or to be truly generative. We know a small and potentially innovative business that is just like that. Great ideas, good delivery, but the partners are so busy doing what urgently has to be done that they haven't time to seek the external funding they need, to promote what they do or to expand enough to get the support staff they need to continue doing what they do best. It is precisely because they are so busy that they need to stop and make space instead of continuing to run themselves into the ground.

Coaching is the supreme space-maker. People who take this time out for coaching from a busy day often actually sigh, visibly relax and begin to slow down in their speech and their movements. However important the issue a client brings, a good coach creates space in which it can be examined from a number of angles, in which it can be considered in differing time frames, and above all in which there is leisure to reflect and engage with high-quality attention. It is these occasions that are the seedbeds of being generative, because they foster a more spacious awareness.

As part of a stress-management initiative, Ian was once asked by an international organisation to engage a group of young, high-flying, totally type-A executives in stepping back from their high-pressure work. By giving them a space in which they could experience the value of taking stock about what really mattered to them – rather than just being busy and driven – the employing organisation was helping some of its most promising people to use their skills and their energy more effectively. The effect of this minimal time investment – one hour for the whole group, once a month for six months – was to enhance peoples' personal leverage in their lives. This made them more generative. As they became more generative, so did the organisation.

Thinking differently, making new connections, drawing upon the whole – not just part – of yourself and being playful are at the heart of being generative. Anything that helps you do this will be good news. You may find that particular questions also help shift things towards a more generative dimension. Maybe a simple enquiry like, 'And what else...?' opens things up, or 'But what do you really, really want?' Sometimes getting a quite different perspective will do it: 'If you were a man from Mars looking at this situation, how might it seem to you?' Going into the future can also make people much more generative: 'Imagine you are six months in the future and this difficulty has been solved ... [pause] What has happened?'

How does a coach give people this profound experience of space? In part, through exercising the skills we have described in Section 2; in part, through their own attitudes and behaviour – for instance being a model of calm and focused enquiry that the client can adopt there and then and later learn to replicate for themselves; in part, by exploring the client's issues MultiModally so they have their full richness and are seen in the round.

All of this makes it possible for the client to *experience a difference that makes a difference*. Wise commissioners recognise this when they make it possible for busy employees to take time away from their desks. We worked with an able young man in a finance house, who had asked for coaching because he was almost at the point of leaving. He was good at his job, but his heart wasn't in it because it only called for a small part of who he was. 'I have to look busy all day,' he said. 'There's no space for me to think or to be creative because I can't be seen to stare out of the window.'

'We don't usually provide coaching for people like this but we want to keep him,' said the HR person who commissioned us. 'If we could only give him space it might allow him to find a better overlap between what the firm needs and what his talents really are.' The coaching itself gave him permission to get into a reflective, open, freewheeling state of mind that allowed him to make new connections. He could be curious, explore and experiment, even make mistakes. Then he became much more focused. For the client, provision of coaching had enormous significance. As he put it early on, 'I feel as though my experience matters … I matter … I'm worth investing in.' And that's when he started investing in the company.

What can being generative do for you?

As in so much of this book, what holds true, holds true for coach, commissioner and client. That's why we use the word 'you' throughout in what follows. The benefits of being generative and the kinds of questions that help someone move towards that way of thinking and working, apply to us all.

Generative interventions can bring you systemic change

One businessman we worked with was about 40 pounds overweight. He knew he needed to lose those pounds, but he wasn't inclined to find any more time to fit in an exercise programme. He worked long, hard days and when he got home all he wanted to do was to eat with his family and then collapse into bed before starting again. The coaching space allowed him to access his own solution: 'Eating less is the only answer,' he said. 'Funnily enough, when I eat from a bowl rather than a plate, I'm actually quite satisfied with less.' In the pause that followed it was as though he had heard the solution for the first time. 'That's what I'll do,' he said. 'It may take time, but I know that will make a difference.'

This client had just invented portion control for himself. And that's totally different from being given the idea as advice by another person. In the weeks that followed he began to notice that eating less was making him feel lighter. This gave him more energy. With more energy he began to be able to contemplate taking some exercise. He had created his own weight-loss plan easily and organically. The weight came off gradually and stayed off. This gave him a new sense of what he could make happen in his life, which gave rise to some soul searching and eventually a change in career. No more long days and late meals because 'I want to see my children before they grow up.'

To get into this frame you might ask questions like:

- 'In your heart of hearts, where do you feel the problem/solution lies?'

- 'What's the smallest thing you could do that could start to make a difference?'

You get to deal with what's really going on and what really matters

Often when you are under pressure your attention is grabbed by what's immediately in front of you, and you may be so busy dealing with that that you don't address the underlying issues. Coaching requires you to ask yourself bigger questions, so setting the current demands within a larger context and a broader time frame.

When you do this, it becomes much easier to prioritise, to work out what fits with your deeper values and aspirations and what doesn't, and to decide where best to invest your time and energy. By learning to focus in on what matters most, rather than just what's immediately in front of you or what others tell you is most urgent, you get to ensure that your actions match up with your values. This means that you become more at one with yourself, and your energy flows more freely and wholeheartedly into what you do.

To get into this frame you might ask questions like:

- 'What's really going on here?'
- 'What do I really want?'
- 'What's most important?'

To open up a more expansive time frame you might ask:

- 'If time slowed right down now what else might I notice about the current situation?'

You can reappraise past beliefs, present behaviours and future aspirations

When you're locked into the pressure of present necessities, you can't consider them in perspective. Coaching helps you to develop a greater flexibility in relation to time. It offers you the opportunity of exploring how what you're doing right now will shape what happens in the future: is it going to get in your way or help you achieve what you want?

To get into this frame, you might look to other areas of your life and ask questions like:

- 'Is there some other place in your life where you find it easier to do what you need to do here?'

Equally, you might want to use others as resources and ask questions like:

- 'Do you know someone else who has the skills you need?'

- 'How would they manage this situation?'

- 'Who is the person that you most admire? What advice might they give you right now?'

You can become more productive

Have you ever had one of those days when you did a lot – but at the end of the day wondered what you'd really achieved? You can be active yet totally unproductive. Activity and productivity are quite different. In our experience coaching frequently first helps people differentiate between these and then reduce the kind of activity that is just busy-ness. As people spend more time on what is more meaningful, more satisfying and more worthy of their commitment and effort, so they become more productive.

What is it to be truly productive? It's to make meaningful progress towards a goal that you consider to be clear and significant. This process has you aligned between what you are doing (*behaviour*) in its immediate and wider context (*environment*), making use of, perhaps even extending, your knowledge and skills (*capabilities*) in a way that furthers what you hold important (*beliefs and values*) and expresses or enhances who you are (*identity*) in line with your wider purpose (*beyond identity*). What you achieve by your activity takes you further at every Logical Level. No wonder it feels so good!

It is also potentially quantifiable. Part of the attraction of coaching is that we can see measurable improvements in performance. Research on the efficacy of coaching is now well under way.

You can improve teamwork dramatically

Being generative will almost certainly involve you in engaging with others to achieve your goals. These people become in some sense your team. Some are formally ratified as teams in organisations, but many exist outside and are virtual. Don't just think of teams as being a work phenomenon, either. It can be very illuminating to view your family, friends or social networks in this light, too.

A team, of course, is a system. When you think and work systemically you can add value to others and derive benefit from them: you achieve more with less. The generative sparking of links between team members can mirror the linking that happens in the brain itself. A good team – be it your family, friends or colleagues – means that what you get is more than the sum of the individuals involved. To get into this frame you might ask yourself questions like:

- Who's on my team? How well are we playing together?

- What am I putting in, taking out and giving up by being a 'team player'?

- Am I really being a team player?

- What benefits do we get from being a team?

- What are our team's values?

- Which members of my team can I rely on in a crisis?

- What are the rules my team plays by? Do we have set plays, or are we free to improvise?

- Is my team generous with its praise and support, or competitive and grudging?

Some systems, like the old Soviet Union, discourage this unregulated linking and ultimately pay the price. This can also happen within a single person, where rigid self-control and the denial of the more unruly or less logical parts of the personality result in personal stagnation or sterility. Curiously enough, it's only when you make an ally of these more anarchic impulses or individuals within personal or organisational teams that they cease to be a threat. That's also when so often they turn out to be one of your greatest assets. Coaching can offer both the space to explore ways of working in this more generative way and strategies for building high-performance teams with divergent characters and qualities.

Just *how* does excellent coaching achieve all this?

It enables you to be generative in *your* way. There isn't just one way. Coaching can adjust to the individual style and needs of each client. Instead of being an off-the-peg training it offers a bespoke experience. Being generative can be promoted in many ways. Sometimes a different way of understanding and approaching things is all that's needed. At other times a more architectural approach is needed, where by using the building materials of existing skill sets, coach and client design new constructs that build into something astonishingly different from what the client has built before. (It was, after all, a pile of shells that inspired the Sydney Opera House!) Yet another approach is to start with a blank slate and dream a new dream altogether like the early developers of the Worldwide Web. Any of these approaches can give rise to generative coaching.

▶ **Generative coaching invites you to go beyond what you already know and find comfortable** A generative approach is based on curiosity, investigation and a playful attitude. This allows you to explore imaginatively but safely. Within the coaching space, you can entertain almost any 'what if?' Becoming aware of your in-built assumptions and underlying values makes you realise where you may be limiting yourself, and where you can make changes that take you into your 'stretch zone' of experimentation and new learning. This in turn helps you to develop your ability to become generative. Some questions can take you in this direction. For instance:

- Where might be a place to start?

- How could you experiment with this?

- What assumptions would help you most here?

- How would you advise someone else in your situation?

- Suppose you were to brainstorm some different things you could do... Don't try to be 'realistic', just see what comes.

▶ **By working across all logical levels, generative coaching ensures that you become more aligned** No more doing what you don't believe in: you either find some aspect that you can accept and work to with full commitment, or you start changing tack. No more unthinking acceptance of an unsatisfactory environment – physical or organisational. Like some of our clients you might customise your desk; ask to change station so you are working among colleagues rather than in a room on your own; begin to build networks more proactively to give yourself a wider base for stimulus and support from which to manage things you can't change; become more assertive with your partner, family or friends; or even decide to look for a new personal or work setting entirely.

Instead of continuing to work in your current job because 'it pays the mortgage and suits me well enough', you might begin to ask yourself how this job matches up with what matters to you on the levels of beliefs and values or identity. If it does, just what about it makes it a good fit – and does recognising that it is a good fit make you feel different about continuing? Or perhaps, having taken time to identify your higher level needs, you might feel happier searching out a job that better meets them?

▶ **Generative coaching helps you assess the impact of change** It's important to consider how what you're doing will affect others in your immediate and more extended networks. Good coaching develops your skills for doing this so you can assess systemic effects. Questions that invite you to consider your personal ecology and that of others include:

- Is this in keeping with your sense of self?

- How is this likely to impact the other people involved?

- What implications could there be at other Logical Levels?

- Might there be any undesirable consequences?

Developing new states of mind

Both creativity and innovation are dependent upon the making of new connections – at the levels of ideas, concepts and how-tos. New connections mean new links being forged, perhaps within the mind via synaptic jumps, perhaps between individuals. And these new connections are in turn dependent upon states of mind and body that are spacious, exploratory and playful. While it's true that the pressure of a deadline can be stimulating, too much of this kind of stimulation will inhibit creativity: once pressure escalates beyond a certain point it can lead to panic or paralysis.

Convergent, outcome-directed thinking is processed in one hemisphere of the brain – the left – while associative (linking, creative) thinking is processed in the other – the right. While truly effective people in many fields have the capacity to use both hemispheres with ease, having space and time to allow the mind to work can make all the difference. Do you ever find that ideas come to you in the shower, or when driving or walking? Times like these, when you are occupied but at a relatively untaxing level, can help you become mentally ambidextrous.

If you want to become more generative, you need to encourage and even create spaces where playful, receptive, associative states can bring your creativity to the fore. This is one reason why we wrote *Your Inner Coach*: we wanted to detail the how-tos, the many straightforward ways in which each of us can enhance our creativity, productivity and well-being. But we also wanted to show that the beauty of this way of working is that it doesn't take up huge amounts of time. In the right circumstances, a bright (or even brilliant) idea can come in a flash: this kind of thinking happens with the lightning speed of natural associative what-if mental connections, not with the careful working out that characterises deductive reasoning.

Neither creativity nor innovation requires originality. Too many people confuse creativity with originality, and as a consequence label themselves 'not creative'. When you think about it, it's really unlikely that anyone will be truly creative in the exact sense of making an object or inventing an idea for the *very first time*. Even Einstein, so often acclaimed as a creative genius, was heavily dependent upon work that others had done before him. As another genius, Isaac Newton, said, 'If I have gone further than others it is only because I have stood on the shoulders of giants.'

When you come down to it, creativity is about new connections, new perspectives, different understandings and different approaches. And we can all produce those when we have space, encouragement, reason and motivation to do so. Coaching can offer us all of these: just as importantly, it can teach us how to offer them to ourselves.

To become generative is to widen your horizons, to take a larger view and to be more inclusive in your thinking and your behaviour. As a result, you can gain new perspectives, new ideas and new allies – and new ways to move forward personally and professionally. You're likely to have greater positive influence throughout the systems you are involved in. Simply setting out to 'fix' a problem is unlikely to open these horizons for you. But coaching that works flexibly and seamlessly across many dimensions can open the way to a wider world – and give you the skills to make that wider world feel like home.

Chapter Thirteen

Dealing with Interference

Remember, resistance can merely mean the forces that operate to keep things in place ... It can be highly productive to encourage your clients to imagine the resistance that could sink their initiatives. This includes their internal resistance as well.

Mary Beth O'Neill, *Executive Coaching with Backbone and Heart*, Jossey-Bass, 2002, pages 122–3

You are committed to your coaching. As the coach, you have an understanding of how to use the essential nuts and bolts. As the commissioner, you have matched the coach and client to the best of your ability and briefed them as well as you know how. As the client, you know your priorities and how to act upon them. So what could go wrong? Plenty, of course, for coaching involves change, and wherever there is change in one part of a system there will be consequences – both actual and anticipated – for other parts. This seems more obvious when the system in question is organisational or interpersonal. But it also happens when change is intra-psychic. Part of the client may sincerely want to make a change, but other parts may not be so willing to accommodate. They may even object.

Not surprisingly, this phenomenon is often referred to as resistance. But it also has other names like blocking, undermining and even sabotage – all judgemental and emotionally loaded descriptions. In our experience, though, such resistance is an understandable and some-times potentially useful response. We are therefore using a more value-neutral term to describe it – to us it's just interference. 'Interference' literally means something that is 'brought, or put, between'.

Change is a dynamic process: having to engage with change, whether it comes from outside or from some part of yourself, prompts dynamic responses. Many of our internal systems are based upon moni-toring and seeking to maintain the status quo – they embody the principle of homeostasis. For example, when you get hot, you automat-ically sweat to cool yourself through evaporation and your surface blood vessels expand to lose heat via convection; when you get cold, you shiver to generate surface heat, while your blood vessels contract and retreat further from the body's surface so as to minimise heat loss. We can get further in anticipating, avoiding or managing interference when we think of it as a natural, potentially adaptive, response like these. These are systemic balancing feedback loops like the ones described in Chapter 3. In short, interference is just feedback from the system. It helps highlight what needs attending to if change is to be successfully implemented.

Interference is *not* a mindless, automatic attempt to protect the status quo. It is there for a reason. It always makes sense – from some perspec-tive. It may be very desirable for someone to lose excess weight as far as they're concerned, but many times we've seen families and friends sabo-tage the process. 'Go on, just one more won't hurt you.' 'I made them specially – I know you like them.' 'You can't be good every day . . .'

Would-be slimmers seeking to understand responses like these by imaginatively stepping into other people's shoes have often been surprised to realise that the fat person others have got used to may be more comfortable or less challenging to live with than the thin one threatening to replace them. And when a slimmer somehow keeps putting off their good intentions for another day and begins to check in with themselves as to why this might be, they can be equally surprised to recognise that if being slim means becoming more attractive, or more in competition with friends or teenage children, there may be good reason for holding themselves back from what seems so 'obviously' a change for the better.

Similar things can happen in organisations. We knew of a business in which the central management had decided upon some important changes in procedure aimed at improving efficiency and competitive edge. So branches of the business were told what to do and given a deadline for implementation. Some responded enthusiastically, retrained their staff and soon had the new procedures in place. But others lost the paperwork or were so busy that they didn't have time to arrange staff training. Come the deadline, they were still operating as before.

When a team came from head office to investigate, they were met with responses like: 'Our customers wouldn't feel they mattered to us as much if we did it that way'; 'Our core staff have all been here for more than 15 years and they're really used to doing it the old way'; 'If we changed now there would be chaos while we got used to the new system and customer service would suffer'; 'We can't afford to lose our regular customers.'

The proposed changes seemed to run counter to things that mattered to them: delaying and effectively refusing to implement the changes was about defending values which the staff held dear. Only by understanding this and taking time to fathom how the changes could actually be implanted while serving, rather than eroding, these key values was management able to get these 'resistant' staff on board.

Interference can take various behavioural forms, from clear-cut opposition at one end of the spectrum to subtle delaying tactics at the other. It can involve a range of emotions, including ambivalence, hostility, fear, self-doubt and anxiety. The mechanisms by which it operates can include limiting beliefs, perfectionism and manipulation. In short, it's a creature of many colours and many disguises. From a coaching perspective, you are likely to encounter three types of interference:

1. Interpersonal.

2. Intra-psychic.

3. Organisational.

Interpersonal interference

This is the kind we tend to think of first. Conflict between people can be obvious and is certainly familiar. You try to do something and others block you. Or you successfully take an initiative – only to be surprised by the force of others' negative responses after the event.

However, interpersonal interference can often be most effectively addressed by sorting out intra-psychic and organisational interference. If you're having difficulties with a particular individual, be it at work or in your personal life, your greatest leverage will probably come from sorting out what you're doing on the inside when you think about this person. Change this and the way you're coming across will change. Every relationship is a self-reinforcing system. Change one element in the system – in this case the one you really do have control over, namely yourself – and the system has to adjust regardless of whether it's intending to or not. Coaching of course can help you do this.

Intra-psychic interference

This is where interference happens within the complex interrelating systems of the self, both mental and physical. Any of us can effectively prevent, limit or sabotage our own achievements in this way – and again, there will always be good reasons why we do this.

This interference can be exclusively internal or play out in how we inhibit ourselves interpersonally. Indeed, what many people think of as interpersonal interference often involves a large measure of self-interference: being fearful of others' reactions, you hold yourself back; anticipating resistance, hostility, criticism or failure, and not wanting to upset people, you put up with the status quo. Here you've short-circuited yourself, but the tendency is often to blame others. Coaching can be a good arena in which to explore the degree of fit between what you expect and what you might actually experience.

Interference that is exclusively intra-psychic can take place in a number of different ways. Below we've listed the most common, and how you might best manage them:

▶ **When different parts of you are in conflict because they want different things.** Unpack and articulate what each part wants, and what it is trying to achieve. There will always be some positive intent for even the most apparently pointless, self-destructive or irrational behaviour or thinking patterns. Honouring that intention by seeking more currently appropriate ways of satisfying these same needs is the key to success. So, the behaviours change but they remain in the service of that positive intent.

▶ **Where you have internalised important values or precepts from others** (usually authority figures such as parents, teachers, experts and mentors), and continue to act on them automatically – but actually they're at odds with what you really believe. Surfacing the belief into words often allows you to recognise not only that it is derived from someone else, but also to change its status from 'must be obeyed' to 'have a choice'. It can also allow you to recognise where something that was appropriate in past circumstances now needs updating. All this reduces the credibility of these previously authoritative utterances.

▶ **Where there is an internal conflict between the drive towards change** (initiative, development, challenge, risk) **on the one hand, and safety on the other** (keeping things the same, sticking to what you know, avoiding risk, continuing to do what you already know you can do). As a result you hedge your bets, get stuck, feel pulled in different directions, or act inconsistently by flip-flopping between going for change and playing it safe.

The key issue here is how you can honour both polarities, as both are essential for healthy living. Successful negotiation rests on clarifying the parties' wants and needs and finding means whereby these can be satisfied. The same applies intra-psychically. Numerous techniques exist. Good coaches will be familiar with both this fundamental principle and the particular tools to implement it.

▶ **Where your body enacts a doubt or a fear that you have not consciously recognised** – for instance, you find you're not able to sleep easily, or you prove unduly susceptible to everyday ailments. (Just too many colds are coming your way, say.) Learning to pay attention to what's bugging you and then addressing it is the best remedy. Initially, this may involve having the physical symptoms and then unpacking what gave rise to them afterwards. The next step is to shorten the feedback loop so that you get into a pattern of self-monitoring that's sensitive to underlying doubt or conflict *before*, not just after, events.

Physical symptoms can also provide an acceptable reason for caution or withdrawal where someone's conscious intent would otherwise drive them, exhaust them or put them at emotional risk. Weekend illnesses, for instance, can sometimes be a necessary protection for someone who is too conscientious and who would otherwise just keep going at the same frenetic pace. The remedy? Have the humility to listen to your body.

Organisational interference

Once you consider an organisation as a single organism, you can recognise that these intra-psychic processes are not confined to individuals. Organisations exhibit their own version. Many years ago, Donald Schon described how large corporations and even national institutions often respond to proposed innovation with what he called 'dynamic conservatism' by shelving, postponing or otherwise resisting the changes. Other studies have demonstrated how large corporations can effectively recreate parent-child patterns of relationships within their staff hierarchies, thus effectively disempowering and infantilising a substantial proportion of their workforce.

Why does this happen? Organisations are made up of people. The structures that govern daily interaction effectively create patterned habits of interpersonal behaviour. These naturally reflect not only the features of deliberate and conscious interaction, but also the unconscious ones. In coaching, this is a dimension that all parties need to be very aware of. Because it operates at an intra-psychic level, it is often not spotted or openly discussed. Sometimes when a coach raises these kinds of issues, people may be dismissive, get defensive or level accusations of 'over-psychologising'. But what is unconscious is out of our normal awareness and it is possible to bring it into conscious awareness. To do so is not to over-psychologise: it is to reclaim our power to shape our own destiny.

Coaching can often help people identify and explore problems arising from this dimension of the organisation, and to develop strategies for managing them more effectively even where overt discussion would not be possible. For example, an organisation often has quite unrealistic expectations of what a newly appointed CEO, senior manager or team leader will achieve. (This also happens in the political arena.) It's almost as though by their very coming the new person will solve problems, set things right and provide a new sense of direction. The organisation is pinning its collective hopes upon this high-status newcomer, but such magical thinking invariably leads to disappointment.

Not surprisingly, the reality turns out to be less glorious. Maybe the new boss achieves some of what's hoped for, but doesn't quite fit the bill in other ways. The dashing of unrealistic hopes can produce an equally exaggerated response of dissatisfaction, and even anger. A key signal for the coach, commissioner and client that this kind of unconscious and collective organisational projection is going on is that the feelings and reactions don't match the reality. The new boss is 'useless'; his ideas are 'rubbish'; he 'hasn't got what it takes'. If the client happens to be the new boss, or one of her subordinates, this can be incredibly undermining. However, if the commissioner or coach understands what's going on, they can assist the client in identifying which concerns do properly rest with her and which ones have just been hung on her. They still need managing, but this can be done from a stronger base of identity.

The central message of coaching is that individuals can learn to manage themselves more effectively and become leaders in their own lives. At times this means finding creative and non-adversarial ways to work within the unseen structural straightjacket of a department, a firm or an industry. At a micro-level, people can often learn to develop more creative and individual strategies for working within infantilising or limiting relationships, and to discriminate between behaviour that helps them reclaim their power and own themselves, and other behaviour that would create unwanted conflict, distress or disruption amongst those they value.

Organisations are particularly adept at generating interference by instituting change on a short-term, narrow-focused remedial basis. Taking the short-term, 'fixing' view of solving problems like this can often result in interference with longer-term, systemic implications. For example, a large school we knew was criticised by its immediate neighbours because of vandalism and bad behaviour by older pupils during the lunch hour. The school's response was to shorten the lunch hour rather than to address the causes of the behaviour. But a shorter lunch hour meant that the children finished school earlier, and all that happened was that the bad behaviour was shifted into the newly lengthened after-school time. Policing measures that seek to address problems of non-compliance in the workplace – for example, signing in, or docking pay for absences – can also run the risk of addressing the symptom rather than the possible underlying causes.

Working with interference

The interference grid

Using our MultiModal model enables commissioner, coach and client to identify which Logical Levels are involved in ongoing or anticipated interference, to what degree it is interpersonal or intra-personal, and how much pertains to the individual and how much to the system. Being clear about the kind of interference you're dealing with like this can help you target your intervention strategies accurately and appropriately. Begin by reminding yourself of the outcome you are seeking, and then use the grid below to identify the type of interference you're experiencing or anticipating.

	Interpersonal	Intra-psychic	Organisational/Systemic
Coach			
Client			
Commissioner			

We've chosen an illustrative example that many coaches and clients will have experienced first-hand.

Lesley has had a long struggle to lose weight. She has been going to a slimming group regularly for the last few months, but after losing a few pounds she has reached a plateau despite 'good' eating habits. Her mother has offered to pay for sessions with a life coach because Lesley doesn't earn much and her husband thinks coaching is a waste of money.

	Interpersonal	Intra-psychic	Organisational/ Systemic
Coach	Lesley's ambivalence means that she tends to change and cancel appointments at short notice.	Do I have any issues that could get in the way here? No.	Aware that helping Lesley achieve her aim may have both long- and short-term consequences within her family and friendship networks
Client (Lesley)	Family tease Lesley and subtly sabotage her attempts to diet and attend her group.	Lesley wants to become thinner, but she has always been the 'fat one' in her family and isn't sure what other issues might surface if she became more successful, assertive and attractive.	Friends are polarised: some encourage her, some others think it's time she stopped being a doormat to her husband. The children are caught up in the conflict between the mother, father and grandmother. They become more difficult to manage as they 'act out' in various ways.
Commissioner (mother)	Lesley's husband thinks she is interfering – as usual – and makes snide remarks.	In conflict about loyalties: should she be supporting her daughter as an independent individual if this means causing tensions within the marriage?	Will helping her daughter in one way cause problems for her in another?

Identifying both your outcome and the type of interference allows you to begin the process of developing appropriate and effective strategies. For example, you might feel that an interpersonal, or even intra-psychic, problem may require an organisational solution. It will also be really useful to consider at what Logical Level the interference is occurring and on what level you can best intervene. Most often, effective interventions take place on a different level to the one on which the problem is being experienced.

When you're seeking the most effective intervention, the leverage you're looking for will need to impact the level of origin – even if your actions are at another level entirely. Too often, though, it's as though the opposite seems to happen. Winning hearts and minds means operating at the level of beliefs, identity and sometimes even beyond, because it's about people's mindsets and attitudes. So, for instance, wanting their people to be more empowered, the organisation puts on a – mandatory! – half-day 'empowerment' programme, where empowerment skills are taught. But this, however, is the wrong Logical Level. This is a capability/behaviour level intervention. It's not just the wrong tool for the job. It's at odds with what's being espoused. It actually threatens to make matters worse because it's likely to engender cynicism in the workforce, who will be acutely aware that this approach doesn't feel right.

The solutions grid

Will interference cease if you or someone else feels differently; if you can take a different attitude; if your thinking changes; if you modify your beliefs in some way? If one of these is involved, we could say you are seeking a solution in the realm of Being.

Will the interference diminish or cease if there's a change in behaviour; if someone does something different or new, or stops doing something? If so, you're looking for a solution in the realm of Doing. So we have two new variables to consider for the interpersonal, the intrapsychic and the organisational. We can represent this thus:

	Being: State, mindset, beliefs	Doing: Activities and behaviour
Interpersonal		
Intra-psychic		
Organisational/ Systemic		

Let's go back to our example:

	Being: State, mindset, beliefs	Doing: Activities and Behaviour
Interpersonal	**Coach** Help client explore and clarify issues, separating out work she can do for and with herself from interpersonal actions and reactions. **Client** Think about what other implications losing weight may have for her as a person, as a wife, as a mother – and as a daughter. What does 'being thinner' involve? **Commissioner** Draw a clear boundary between paying for and owning or driving the results of the coaching.	**Coach** Talk with Lesley about 1. lateness and cancellation as possible signs of ambivalence, and 2. about knock-on effects among family and friends. **Client** Make sure her family know how important losing weight is to her – and reassure them in a variety of ways that this isn't a threat to them. **Commissioner** Discuss issues with Lesley and find non-contentious ways to show support for Lesley's husband and children.
Intra-psychic	**Coach** Remind self that the agenda, and the rate of progress, are Lesley's. 'Success' will be measured in her terms. **Client** Imagine and test out responses to different scenarios and strategies until she finds ones that feel acceptable at every Logical Level. **Commissioner** Find ways to monitor own possible investment in Lesley's progress.	**Client** Review beliefs about being the 'fat one'. Where did they come from? Are they relevant now? Determine what will help avoid rerunning old patterns. Clarify new thinking and self-image. **Commissioner** Encourage daughter in self-reflection and re-evaluation.

Organisational/Systemic	Coach Be mindful of the family's responses and of the need to take these into account when helping the client manage herself and her situation more effectively. Client Think about what it means to be a member of this family and a partner in this marriage – what is given and received, what is expected, what feels right and what doesn't. What are the others likely to be feeling, fearing, wanting?	Coach Help client prioritise, and test out possible strategies from a full range of perspectives before committing herself to action. Client Review friendships. Who is really for her and who isn't? Is she spending time and energy in the best places? Is it time to refresh the relationship with her husband and to create new expectations? Address husband's possible anxieties implicitly through behaviour and where appropriate in words. Commissioner Be scrupulous in avoiding actions that might be taken as interfering within the marriage or family.

It is easy in coaching to focus attention on 'problems' and 'outcomes'. But it is also really valuable to devote some of your attention to exploring what is getting in the way – or what is likely to.

Taking the time to consider just why and how difficulties are arising gives you important information and the means of devising strategies that go beyond struggle. Resistance feeds on struggle. By contrast, if you acknowledge the validity of the concerns it represents and then incorporate these into your proposals, you stop this polarisation. The interference is no longer an obstacle, but an ally. It has alerted you to potential glitches. Address these and you have just strengthened your chance of *sustained* success.

SECTION 4: Coaching and Beyond

Introduction

Coaching has established itself worldwide as a powerful intervention that benefits both individual clients and the organisations they work in. But good coaching leaves a legacy that lasts beyond the immediate issue or decision point that initiated it. This is true for both individuals and teams and it happens in different ways. For one of our clients it was simply that 'I have been heard, so now I can hear myself.' Another put it this way, 'from the outside it may seem that nothing much has changed – but everything has changed for me because I know how to manage myself now.' Sometimes the changes for clients are practical and obvious: 'I take time out every day to attend to myself and my priorities now, and that has created the space I needed. I do a better job and I can leave work at work more than I did before, which means my family is getting more of me.' The same can be true of teams too: 'They came back so much more positive from those very first coaching sessions – and that's continued. The whole team works better now.' Other times a profound reorientation occurs that changes the quality of the life you're living. One client put it this way: 'I had looked enough at the world's pavements. I thought, "what else can I look at?" So I looked at the sky – and started to walk taller.'

Experienced as the dynamic partnership we've been describing, coaching can be truly life-transforming. It initiates learning and change across all Logical Levels. It shifts thinking from a remedial to a generative mindset. It creates a more systemic awareness. It focuses attention on what's going on inside you (the intra-psychic, emotional and somatic) and between you and others. Because of this its approach and the skills you learn become integrated into an enriched way of being. That's what this last section is about.

Chapter Fourteen

From Insight to Action

> *Our basic nature is to act, and not be acted upon. As well as enabling us to choose our response to particular circumstances, this empowers us to create circumstances. Taking initiative does not mean being pushy, obnoxious, or aggressive. It does mean recognising our responsibility to make things happen.*

Stephen R. Covey, *The 7 Habits of Highly Effective People,* Simon & Schuster, 1989,

page 75

Coaching is a process that you engage in through a finite series of interactive experiences, either face to face or via the telephone. Since its term is fixed and sometimes quite short, it's worth thinking of it not just as a self-contained experience, but also as a kick-start to a whole new way of operating. Good coaches know that it has this potential. They'll be fostering this transition from insight to action throughout the coaching contract. As that contract comes towards its end they may well invite clients to reflect on how they are going to customise their learning and take it forward *for themselves.* We'd like to be able to do the same with what you've been learning. That's what this chapter is about.

There is a saying in Papua New Guinea that you don't really know something till you know it 'in the muscle'. Then it's not just in your head: it's really part of you. However exciting an idea, however illuminating an insight or however powerful a strategy you encounter, it remains largely inert until you have made it your own. Until it has changed your thinking and your actions, its value is negligible. As learners as well as trainers, readers as well as writers, clients as well as coaches, we believe that this is the next step. So we want to outline a simple structure that can help you customise what you gain from reading this book. We want your learning to become a part of your personal vocabulary rather than a quotation from us, a tool you reach for rather than a recipe you once read.

As a client, commissioner or coach, you are engaged on a journey that is both professional and personal. We are very aware that to be truly useful, learning has to become part of you: it has to undergo a process of integration so that it can be, as that Papua New Guinea proverb has it, 'in the muscle'. What is going to make this happen? We certainly can't count on it occurring automatically just through reading. However illuminating an idea you read about may be, the experience of reading is not active enough. There's all the difference in the world between thinking: 'What a great idea! What a useful tool! Must remember that!' and it becoming something that naturally informs your thinking and guides your actions. How do you get from the newly informed stage of conscious incompetence (would like to do that but can't yet) to the deliberate, perhaps over-effortful stage of conscious competence, and then beyond that again to the effortless appropriateness of *un*conscious competence?

We want to suggest a process for *self-coaching* that reflects the processes involved in *interpersonal* coaching. Good commissioners and good coaches don't just 'do' coaching to other people – it's a way of engaging that also enriches how they relate to themselves. And clients can build this themselves. These are the steps in the self-coaching process, which are explained in the text that follows:

1. Create a space for yourself.

2. Log on to a more spacious awareness.

3. Change your focal length.

4. Use the change of focus to elicit new information.

5. Clarify what happens next.

Create a space for yourself

Very simply create a space – mental and perhaps also physical – where you can usefully engage with yourself. It will pay huge dividends. There are many ways of doing this detailed in our book *Your Inner Coach* (see page 186). What they all have in common is that they enable you to step out of your habitual framework for a moment, and so create a space between insight and action that makes any action you take thereafter infinitely more powerful.

Log on to a more spacious awareness

We all take many things about ourselves for granted, or deal with them without really assessing what's going on and why. Physical experience can be a good example. There will be times when, like many people, you hunch your shoulders. It might even be a habit. Let's suppose you realise that you're doing this. Normally you'd be likely to try and adjust – you'd move to compensate. However, when people do so they're starting from a tight place and they may strain and *over*compensate.

One of the key principles developed by F.M. Alexander, founder of the Alexander Technique, was that we could notice our habitual responses and learn to momentarily inhibit the desire to change them. Alexander's injunction to inhibit the impulse to act – and to give an internal instruction to oneself to let the neck be free to allow the back to lengthen and widen – can create a profound state change when executed correctly. *Then* when you attend to your shoulders, the spontaneous adjustment that occurs is both astonishingly easy and much more far reaching. In such everyday muscular patterns, poor habits have literally got themselves 'into the muscle'. The momentary inhibiting of action that Alexander taught interrupts the normal stimulus-response pattern and offers a useful model for monitoring many other habits. Noticing while inhibiting action creates a moment's pause – and gives you the opportunity of creating a more spacious awareness. Out of that gap can come new possibilities for the mind to reflect and the body to realign.

To create a more spacious awareness like this is to give yourself the opportunity to reflect and review, redefine and redirect. It may take only seconds. It could take much longer. Without this ability you can end up the victim of your habitual knee-jerk responses, because there's simply no space to make the new connections that you need for a different understanding or a new behaviour.

One of our clients described coaching as 'a space to think', another as 'a space to be'. That space comes from asking the right kinds of questions in the right kind of way at the right kind of time. Done well this creates a profound change in a person's internal state which allows them to engage with themselves and their experience in a quite different way. Here's a way to start.

Change your focal length

We can get so used to looking at things in a certain way that we no longer 'see' what's there. We are likely to be filtering out some information without even intending to, and distorting other information to fit our expectations and existing beliefs. Time to break with old patterns and try something new. Think of a zoom lens. It enables you to get amazing close-ups. However, this very capacity can also distort your understanding of what you're looking at. Remember those kids' competitions where you had to guess what the close-up was a picture of? It looked like nothing you'd ever seen and turned out to be something absolutely mundane at 250 magnification. If you're too close you may not recognise what you're dealing with. Playing with focal length can help you test out your existing assumptions and check the potential value of different perspectives on your situation.

Use the change of focus to elicit new information

The trick for the coach is to get into the habit of *eliciting* information that's not been available before. This takes the client much further than either instructing or seeking to install a new behaviour or a new attitude. Ultimately, it's also what the client learns to do for himself. We can all know what we should do, yet be unable to do it or, despite knowing, still revert to old patterns under pressure. Eliciting is like the match that lights the fuse that sets off the firework that blossoms in the night sky and leaves its after-image on the retina and in the mind's eye. Running your situation, your problem or your goals through the different dimensions of our MultiModal model, for example, will help you elicit information that was previously hidden to you, and at the same time help you get the model into your muscle.

Questions are one of the best vehicles for elicitation (see Chapter 7). Of course, there is a fine line between eliciting information and installing new behaviour or attitudes. To ask a question is to direct attention as it sends the listener on a *quest* in a particular internal direction. As the coach, you need a genuinely open mind to avoid suggesting a preference for the client to follow. If you're a client, you might create the space – and this spacious awareness within yourself – to ask yourself good coaching questions. Whether you're the commissioner, coach or client, asking questions that direct attention to the dimensions of the MultiModal model will yield information without being prescriptive. Here are some other suggestions:

- What are my optimal conditions for learning?

- Am I confusing what I do with who I am?

- How would it be to feel that I can change my views, my skills or my behaviour and still remain 'me'?

- How much easier would it feel for me to change if I were to take external comments as feedback rather than as badges of 'success' or 'failure'?

- What are my strengths and how can I play to them?

- What's within my comfort zone – and what might be a step I could now take to stretch me?

As a coach, you might also ask yourself:

- What is the issue here?

- What is my outcome here?

- What's the point of the question I am about to ask?

- What's the smallest intervention I can make that will give the leverage I'm seeking?

- How can I stay out of the client's way?

- What would be a useful stretch for this person?

Clarify what happens next

This is the final stage, where you take the information you have gathered through the process and translate it into action. Questions that can prompt this include:

- So what?

- What's next?

- What's the first step I can take?

- What's needed?

- How can I put my learning into practice?

How can using this process change your life?

Arguably you cannot move forward at all without first creating a space. You cannot find a new idea, a new truth or a new way without first being willing to create what Coleridge called that 'willing suspension of disbelief' – to be ready to say to yourself 'what if?' To do that you need both to know and to be willing to temporarily suspend the idea, the truth and the way that you have become habituated to. When you do this, you may begin to see yourself in a new way, as a self-organising construct not as a fixed and finite entity – what Carl Rogers described as 'an integrated process of changingness'.

To think of oneself like this can be scary, or liberating and exciting – sometimes both. Just like coaching. However, recognising that neither we nor others are ever 'fixed' or finished, means that it is never too late to learn, to change, to grow, to say sorry, to let something go or to take something up. This ongoing engagement in the process of living and being is a characteristic of people who live long and enjoy being alive. It shares many of the characteristics of children's play: intent yet light-hearted; opening up more options rather than closing them and focusing in on just a few; being willing to explore different avenues and be guided by experience as to which one feels right, rather than allowing it to be prescribed and proscribed. It is about being human and humane, rather than a learning automaton. The coach's job is to foster this kind of experience.

Coaching is about engaging in the process of enquiry, living its spirit rather than following its letter. Our hope is that you're engaging not just with our ideas but also with *yourself*. To the extent that you do, you can continue to discover, enjoy and even be surprised by what is within you.

Chapter Fifteen

Living the Spirit of Coaching

This, I believe, is the great Western truth: That each of us is a completely unique creature, and that, if we are ever to give any gift to the world, it will have to come out of our own experience and fulfilment of our own potentialities, not someone else's.

Joseph Campbell, *The Hero's Adventure*, Broadway Books, 1988, page 151

Coaching is not about techniques for doing but skills for being. That's why so much of what we have been exploring applies to whatever role you're in. Coaching is a way of viewing both oneself and others. It rests on fundamental assumptions:

- Human beings are resourceful.

- People have a much greater ability to understand and direct themselves when they are invited to explore and reflect with curiosity and without judgement.

- You can help others best by assisting them to stay engaged and focused, and by encouraging them to ask powerful questions that stimulate internal search.

- No one exists in isolation. We are involved with others as part of many different systems, be they family, friendships, formal organisations, informal groupings, specific cultures or even nations. The interplay between these is dynamic and mutually influential.

- As individuals, we are also made up of interconnecting systems: mind and body, intellect and emotion, reflection and action, muscular, organic, cellular. Conscious processing is only part of the story: we also need to draw upon the wisdom of the body and the understanding of the unconscious mind.

- When you cultivate an attitude of respect and curiosity about yourself, about others and about the systems in which you are involved, you rapidly begin to wonder, and then to marvel. You begin to enter a state of reverence. Wonder and reverence are the foundations for a life led in the spirit of coaching.

- Techniques can be good tools if skilfully applied, but like all tools they are only effective at the right places and in the right times. They are valuable servants but poor masters.

- The best use of a tool is not solely to assist in the completion of a task but also to open opportunities for leading a better life.

- Coaching that delivers what's expected may be useful: coaching that delivers something beyond expectation may be more useful still.

- If you regard yourself and others with wonder and reverence you will more readily seek explanations for what disappoints or doesn't work, and you will open avenues rather than close doors.

Living in the spirit of coaching is to cultivate an ongoing awareness that is sensitive and fresh, that acknowledges frustration and lack of fit as a signal for possible change, and that celebrates lightness of heart, the joy of committed involvement and the power of playfulness. It deconstructs the clichés that there's no gain without pain, that there have to be winners and losers, that 'better' and 'worse' relate to measurable external criteria or benchmarks, that effort has to feel effortful and that work and play are opposites. It rests not on a blind optimism that all is well, or 'she'll be right', but on a well-founded faith that in spite of disappointments, setbacks and disasters, in spite of anger and frustration, misunderstandings and brutality, we have, as both individuals and as social beings, the means to enjoy life and to make it worth living.

Above all, the spirit of coaching helps you move from a preoccupation with everyday necessities to a sense of how even the routine or mundane can, if viewed in a different light, give us cause to wonder and marvel. It's all a matter of using your senses freshly and allowing yourself to encounter familiar things and happenings as if you were a stranger to the planet and its ways. And in fact, that's quite near to the truth.

For all the advances in knowledge that amaze and benefit us, we can now be quite sure that at least 85 per cent of the universe is still completely unknown to us. The universe we can see and sense is but a fraction of what is 'out there' – no more than 15 per cent in fact. The rest is made up of what astrophysicists now call dark matter. Its properties are hard to even conceptualise, let alone to understand. Although we know it has to be there, because of the behaviour of the observable universe, right now its presence can only be inferred.

Yet perhaps the darkest of dark matter is to be found within the very brain that can recognise the existence of something that goes beyond what it's yet able to know. To be prepared to do that, and to then take delight in doing it and experience the awe that comes with seeing its fruits, is to live in the spirit of coaching.

Appendix

The following account of the core coaching competencies was developed by the International Coach Federation. It can be found on the ICF website (www.coach federation.org) and is reproduced with permission.

Coaching Core Competencies

The following eleven core coaching competencies were developed to support greater understanding about the skills and approaches used within today's coaching profession as defined by the ICF. They will also support you in calibrating the level of alignment between the coach-specific training expected and the training you have experienced.

Finally, these competencies were used as the foundation for the ICF Credentialing process examination.

The core competencies are grouped into four clusters according to those that fit together logically based on common ways of looking at the competencies in each group. The groupings and individual competencies are not weighted – they do not represent any kind of priority in that they are all core or critical for any competent coach to demonstrate.

A. Setting the Foundation

1. meeting ethical guidelines and professional standards
2. establishing the coaching agreement

B. Co-creating the Relationship

3. establishing trust and intimacy with the client
4. coaching presence

C. Communicating Effectively

5. active listening
6. powerful questioning
7. direct communication

D. Facilitating Learning and Results

8. creating awareness
9. designing actions
10. planning and goal setting
11. managing progress and accountability

NOTE: Each competency listed on the following pages has a definition and related behaviours. Behaviours are classified as either those that should always be present and visible in any coaching interaction, or those that are called for in certain coaching situations and, therefore, not always visible in any one coaching interaction.

ICF Core Competencies and Demonstrations

Meeting Ethical Guidelines and Professional Standards

Coach demonstrates an understanding of coaching ethics and standards and the ability to apply them appropriately in the coaching relationship.

Establishing the Coaching Agreement

Coach demonstrates an ability to understand what is required in the specific coaching interaction and to come to agreement with the client about the coaching process and the coaching relationship.

Establishing Trust and Intimacy with the Client

Coach demonstrates an ability to create a safe, supportive environment that produces ongoing mutual respect and trust.

Coaching Presence

Coach demonstrates an ability to be fully conscious and create spontaneous relationship with the client employing a style that is open, flexible and confident.

Active Listening

Coach demonstrates an ability to focus completely on what the client is saying and is not saying, to understand the meaning of what is said in the context of the client's desires, and to support client self-expression.

Powerful Questioning

Coach demonstrates an ability to ask questions that reveal the information needed for maximum benefit for the coaching relationship and for the client.

Direct Communication

Coach demonstrates an ability to communicate effectively during coaching sessions, and to use language that has the greatest positive impact on the client.

Creating Awareness

Coach demonstrates an ability to integrate and accurately evaluate multiple sources of information and to make interpretations that help the client to gain awareness and thereby achieve agreed-upon results.

Designing Actions

Coach demonstrates an ability to create, with the client, opportunities for ongoing learning during coaching and in work or life situations, and for taking new actions that will most effectively lead to agreed-upon coaching results.

Planning and Goal Setting

Coach demonstrates an ability to develop and maintain an effective coaching plan with the client.

Managing Progress and Accountability

Coach demonstrates an ability to hold attention on what is important for the client and to leave responsibility with the client to take action.

A. Setting the Foundation

1. ▶ **Meeting Ethical Guidelines and Professional Standards** – Understanding of coaching ethics and standards and ability; to apply them appropriately in all coaching situations
   a. Understands and exhibits in own behaviours the ICF Standards of Conduct
   b. Understands and follows all ICF Ethical Guidelines
   c. Clearly communicates the distinctions between coaching, consulting, psychotherapy and other support professions
   d. Refers client to another support professional as needed, knowing when this is needed and the available resources.
2. ▶ **Establishing the Coaching Agreement** – Ability to understand what is required in the specific coaching interaction and to come to agreement with the prospective and new client about the coaching process and relationship
   a. Understands and effectively discusses with the client the guidelines and specific parameters of the coaching relationship (e.g. logistics, fees, scheduling, inclusion of others if appropriate)
   b. Reaches agreement about what is appropriate in the relationship

and what is not, what is and is not being offered, and about the client's and coach's responsibilities

c. Determines whether there is an effective match between his/her coaching method and the needs of the prospective client.

B. Co-Creating the Relationship

3. ▶ **Establishing Trust and Intimacy with the Client** – Ability to create a safe supportive environment that produces ongoing mutual respect and trust

a. Shows genuine concern for the client's welfare and future

b. Continuously demonstrates personal integrity, honesty and sincerity

c. Establishes clear agreements and keeps promises

d. Demonstrates respect for client's perceptions, learning style, personal being

e. Provides ongoing support for and champions new behaviours and actions, including those involving risk taking and fear of failure

f. Asks permission to coach client in sensitive, new areas.

4. ▶ **Coaching Presence** – Ability to be fully conscious and create spontaneous relationship with the client, employing a style that is open, flexible and confident

a. Is present and flexible during the coaching process, dancing in the moment

b. Accesses own intuition and trusts one's inner knowing – "goes with the gut"

c. Is open to not knowing and takes risks

d. Sees many ways to work with the client, and chooses in the moment what is most effective

e. Uses humour effectively to create lightness and energy

f. Confidently shifts perspectives and experiments with new possibilities for own action

g. Demonstrates confidence in working with strong emotions, and can self-manage and not be overpowered or enmeshed by client's emotions.

Communicating Effectively

5. ▶ **Active Listening** – Ability to focus completely on what the client is saying and is not saying, to understand the meaning of what is said in the context of the client's desires, and to support client self-expression

   a. Attends to the client and the client's agenda, and not to the coach's agenda for the client

   b. Hears the client's concerns, goals, values and beliefs about what is and is not possible

   c. Distinguishes between the words, the tone of voice, and the body language

   d. Summarises, paraphrases, reiterates, mirrors back what client has said to ensure clarity and understanding

   e. Encourages, accepts, explores and reinforces the client's expression of feelings, perceptions, concerns, beliefs, suggestions, etc.

   f. Integrates and builds on client's ideas and suggestions

   g. "Bottom-lines" or understands the essence of the client's communication and helps the client get there rather than engaging in long descriptive stories

   h. Allows the client to vent or "clear" the situation without judgement or attachment in order to move on to next steps.

6. ▶ **Powerful Questioning** – Ability to ask questions that reveal the information needed for maximum benefit to the coaching relationship and the client

   a. Asks questions that reflect active listening and an understanding of the client's perspective

   b. Asks questions that evoke discovery, insight, commitment or action (e.g. those that challenge the client's assumptions)

   c. Asks open-ended questions that create greater clarity, possibility or new learning

   d. Asks questions that move the client towards what they desire, not questions that ask for the client to justify or look backwards.

7. ▶ **Direct Communication** – Ability to communicate effectively during coaching sessions, and to use language that has the greatest positive impact on the client

   a. Is clear, articulate and direct in sharing and providing feedback

b. Reframes and articulates to help the client understand from another perspective what he/she wants or is uncertain about
c. Clearly states coaching objectives, meeting agenda, purpose of techniques or exercises
d. Uses language appropriate and respectful to the client (e.g. non-sexist, non-racist, non-technical, non-jargon)
e. Uses metaphor and analogy to help to illustrate a point or paint a verbal picture.

D. Facilitating Learning and Results

8. ▶ **Creating Awareness** – Ability to integrate and accurately evaluate multiple sources of information, and to make interpretations that help the client to gain awareness and thereby achieve agreed-upon results

a. Goes beyond what is said in assessing client's concerns, not getting hooked by the client's description
b. Invokes inquiry for greater understanding, awareness and clarity
c. Identifies for the client his/her underlying concerns, typical and fixed ways of perceiving himself/herself and the world, differences between the facts and the interpretation disparities between thoughts, feelings and action
d. Helps clients to discover for themselves the new thoughts, beliefs, perceptions, emotions, moods, etc. that strengthen their ability to take action and achieve what is important to them
e. Communicates broader perspectives to clients and inspires commitment to shift their viewpoints and find new possibilities for action
f. Helps clients to see the different, interrelated factors that affect them and their behaviours (e.g. thoughts, emotions, body, background)
g. Expresses insights to clients in ways that are useful and meaningful for the client
h. Identifies major strengths vs. major areas for learning and growth, and what is most important to address during coaching
i. Asks the client to distinguish between trivial and significant issues, situational vs. recurring behaviours, when detecting a separation between what is being stated and what is being done

9. ▶ **Designing Actions** – Ability to create with the client opportunities for ongoing learning, during coaching and in work/life situations, and for taking new actions that will most effectively lead to agreed-upon coaching results

   a. Brainstorms and assists the client to define actions that will enable the client to demonstrate, practice and deepen new learning
   b. Helps the client to focus on and systematically explore specific concerns and opportunities that are central to agreed-upon coaching goals
   c. Engages the client to explore alternative ideas and solutions, to evaluate options, and to make related decisions
   d. Promotes active experimentation and self-discovery, where the client applies what has been discussed and learned during sessions immediately afterwards in his/her work or life setting
   e. Celebrates client successes and capabilities for future growth
   f. Challenges client's assumptions and perspectives to provoke new ideas and find new possibilities for action
   g. Advocates or brings forward points of view that are aligned with client goals and, without attachment, engages the client to consider them
   h. Helps the client "Do It Now" during the coaching session, providing immediate support
   i. Encourages, stretches and challenges, but also at a comfortable pace of learning.

10. ▶ **Planning and Goal Setting** – Ability to develop and maintain an effective coaching plan with the client

   a. Consolidates collected information and establishes a coaching plan and development goals with the client that address concerns and major areas for learning and development
   b. Creates a plan with results that are attainable, measurable, specific and have target dates
   c. Makes plan adjustments as warranted by the coaching process and by changes in the situation
   d. Helps the client identify and access different resources for learning (e.g. books, other professionals)
   e. Identifies and targets early successes that are important to the client.

11. ▶ **Managing Progress and Accountability** – Ability to hold attention on what is important for the client, and to leave responsibility with the client to take action

  a. Clearly requests of the client actions that will move the client towards their stated goals

  b. Demonstrates follow through by asking the client about those actions that the client committed to during the previous session(s)

  c. Acknowledges the client for what they have done, not done, learned or become aware of since the previous coaching session(s)

  d. Effectively prepares, organises and reviews with client information obtained during sessions

  e. Keeps the client on track between sessions by holding attention on the coaching plan and outcomes, agreed-upon courses of action, and topics for future session(s)

  f. Focuses on the coaching plan but is also open to adjusting behaviours and actions based on the coaching process and shifts in direction during sessions

  g. Is able to move back and forth between the big picture of where the client is heading, setting a context for what is being discussed and where the client wishes to go

  h. Promotes client's self-discipline and holds the client accountable for what they say they are going to do, for the results of an intended action, or for a specific plan with related time frames

  i. Develops the client's ability to make decisions, address key concerns, and develop himself/herself (to get feedback, to determine priorities and set the pace of learning, to reflect on and learn from experiences)

  j. Positively confronts the client with the fact that he/she did not take agreed-upon actions.

Bibliography

The number of books on coaching seems to be increasing exponentially. We have confined ourselves to suggesting a few titles which we believe will offer a useful way in to anyone wanting to explore further and which are true to the spirit of the enterprise that is coaching.

Buckingham, Marcus & Clifton, Donald, *Now, Discover Your Strengths*, Free Press Business, 2002

Flaherty, James, *Coaching: Evoking Excellence in Others*, Butterworth Heinemann, 1999

Gallwey, W. Timothy, *The Inner Game of Tennis*, Random House, 1994

Gallwey, W. Timothy, *The Inner Game of Work*, Random House, 2000

Kline, Nancy, *Time to Think: listening to ignite the human mind*, Ward Lock, 1999

Leonard, Thomas J., *The Portable Coach*, Scribner, 1998

McDermott, Ian & Jago, Wendy, *The NLP Coach*, Piatkus, 2001

McDermott, Ian & Jago, Wendy, *Your Inner Coach*, Piatkus, 2003

O'Neill, Mary Beth, *Executive Coaching with Backbone and Heart*, Jossey-Bass, 2000

O'Connor, Joseph, & McDermott, Ian, *The Art of Systems Thinking*, Thorsons, 1997

Senge, Peter, M. *The Fifth Discipline*, Century Business, 1990

Silsbee, Douglas K., *The Mindful Coach: Seven Roles for Helping People Grow*, Ivy River Press, 2004

Whitmore, John, *Coaching for Performance*, Nicholas Brealey, 1992

Whitworth, Laura, Kimsey-House Henry & Sandahl, Phil, *Co-active Coaching*, Davies-Black, 1998.

Resources

Contacting the authors

We welcome your feedback and are also available for coaching.

Contact Ian McDermott at:
Tel: 01268 777125
Website: www.itsnlp.com

Contact Wendy Jago at:
Tel: 01273 492848
Email: wendy@jagoconsulting.eclipse.co.uk

International Coaching Bodies

If you want to explore further afield we suggest checking out the websites of the International Coach Federation and the European Mentoring and Coaching Council.

For up to date information on coaching organisations and their approaches see:

International Coach Federation
Website: www.coachfederation.org

European Mentoring and Coaching Council
Website: www.emccouncil.org

Next Steps

If you have found this book of interest you will almost certainly enjoy actually working with a coach. You might even think about becoming one yourself eventually.

Finding a Coach

To find a coach who's right for you, you might like to call the ITS office on +44 (0)1268 777125. If you prefer you can email us on coach@ itsnlp.com

With coaching now the flavour of the month, we urge you to be very careful and check out people's credentials. At the present time, it is very much a case of buyer beware. The ICF website is one source of reputable professionals. Of course personal recommendation of a professional by others who have benefited from their skills is another route. If the values and approach outlined in this book speak to you, you might want to contact International Teaching Seminars (ITS), whose Director of Training is Ian McDermott. ITS has pioneered NLP coach training and maintains a directory of fully trained coaches.

Coach Training

ITS has pioneered advanced coaching training and is in active collaboration with leading coaching institutes and trainers in Europe, and in North and South America. It is the world's market leader in NLP Coach training. It offers numerous short courses and also full-length programmes, including Practitioner, Master Practitioner and Coaching Certification training where you can be trained by Ian McDermott and the best international trainers from around the world.

Masterful coaches know that the path to mastery goes on forever, that it is not brilliance but perseverance that brings progress – and that every new peak of achievement is just the prelude to another plateau that will challenge what they thought they'd got figured out!

ITS coach training programmes are designed to support people in their individual and different *journeys toward greater mastery*.

Essential Coaching

This brief programme introduces some of the fundamentals of a coaching approach. (An edited version is available on a 2 CD set).

European NLP Coaching Certification Training

This programme is designed for those who wish to develop a coaching approach or who are interested in a career as an NLP Coach.

The first NLP Coach Training in the world to be recognised by the International Coach Federation (ICF). Successful completion of this training leads to certification as an NLP Coach.

Coaching Mastery Certification Programme

Mastery in coaching has this in common with all mastery – it requires mastery in being and mastery in doing. This advanced programme is for those who seek to pursue their own path to mastery not just as a coach but in life as a whole. A unique feature of this programme is the extraordinary access it gives you to trainers from so many different schools of coaching.

If you are ready for advanced coaching training this programme will give you the tools, the experience and the mentors.

ITS Website

This contains many articles as well as details of all training. For further information on finding a coach or about coach training check out the ITS website.

To reach Ian McDermott or get further information:
Website: www.itsnlp.com

VIP Email List

If you would like to keep abreast of new developments you may want to join our VIP email list. When you join the VIP email list you will:

• Have access to free ITS Teleseminars

• Be invited to special VIP members only events

• Get notification of new programmes before official launch dates

Just go to the website and click on VIP email list.

Alternatively, to receive a free brochure, please call ITS on:
Inside UK: 01268 777125   Fax: 01268 777976
Outside UK: +44 1268 777125   Fax: +44 1268 777976

Or write to:
International Teaching Seminars,
ITS House
Webster Court
Websters Way
Rayleigh
Essex
SS6 8JX
United Kingdom

Index

Coaching Resources

How to Coach Yourself

Coaching is not just about working with other people – you can also use these same coaching skills to successfully coach yourself. Whether you want to plan your career more effectively, have more control over your thoughts and feelings, improve relationships or tackle issues from the past, this CD is designed to give you what you need to be your own best Coach.

Spiritual Dimension of Coaching

While Coaching can provide powerful practical results and change in our lives, it also has the potential to go much, much deeper. On this special CD, Ian McDermott brings together two decades experience to show you how to engage with a more profound level of experience.

The Power to Change

Change: Many people want it but most struggle to achieve it. On this CD, Ian McDermott unveils the secrets of powerful and effective change. By combining the tools of NLP and Coaching you will discover how to break through the limitations that may have been preventing people getting the changes they desired from happening easily.

Essential Coaching Skills

The power of coaching comes not just from the effectiveness of its numerous tools – but also the fact that these are skills that anyone can easily use. As a leading trainer of coaches, one of Ian McDermott's great skills lies in translating coaching into simple steps that you can use immediately to make a profound difference to your life. On this double CD, Ian introduces you to a powerful set of skills that will enable you to assist yourself and others make rapid, lasting change.

The Coach's Toolkit

Have access to the actual materials developed and refined over 10 years by a working Master Certified Coach. Jan Elfline has put together everything that would have made her life so much easier if it had existed when she was starting out. Topics covered include: creating your own intake packet, how to introduce coaching, successful practice management, easy documentation for professional certification, effective training agreements.

www.itsnlp.com